eVolo

**edited by
Carlo Aiello**

SKYSCRAPER FOR THE XXI CENTURY

eVolo Publishing
SKYSCRAPER FOR THE XXI CENTURY

1005866696

Editor: Carlo Aiello
SKYSCRAPER FOR THE XXI CENTURY includes work produced by participants around the world for the 06, 07, and 08 eVolo Skyscraper Competition.

Cover illustration: Chimera
Paula Tomisaki

ISBN-10: 0-9816658-0-2
ISBN-13: 978-0-9816658-0-1

CONTENTS

INTRODUCTION

eVolo Architecture was founded in New York City in 2003. Led by a group of international architects, the goal of the group was to create a forum for the discussion, debate and development of novel architectural design in the XXI Century.

One of the strategies employed by eVolo has been architectural competitions, which have been an immense success on an international scale. The first, which was held in 2005, received submissions from young architects from over sixty nations worldwide to be judged by world-class jurors. We believe that this collision of expertise and innovation is of momentous value to the furthering of the discipline.

In this book we present the top ranked projects from the 06, 07, and 08 Skyscraper Competition. The central conception of these competitions was to speculate as to the reality and future of the skyscraper, posing questions such as; What is the skyscraper in the beginning of the XXI Century? What is the historical and social context of these mega-structures? What is their response to the urban fabric? Is the modern skyscraper a city in and of itself? Is the human scale lost?

The word "skyscraper" was used in the past to refer to big, tall, sailing ships. It was not until the XX Century that the term was used to indicate a tall building. From its Chicago origins to its Asian present, skyscrapers inspire the imagination of millions. Unfortunately, hundreds of new towers have been developed in the past few years without consideration of their environmental and contextual consequences. It has become virtually impossible to distinguish between novelty and innovation. The lack of urban planning and poor architectural design, fueled by a short-term profit approach, has left the world with non-efficient skyscrapers that use large amounts of energy and have conventional spaces without intellectual or perceptual enjoyment.

It is also crucial that we consider the struggle particular to the city, such that it can accommodate ample infrastructure and necessary urban resources. This is most challenging in high density areas where problems such as pollution and traffic congestion are perpetual considerations.

The past few decades have witnessed an architectural race between nations to erect the tallest structures, seen as tangible representations of economic prosperity, technological advancement, and geo-political power. While understandable, this has resulted in a lack of appropriate location-specific considerations, all in the name of insensible architectural display.

Talented architects have entered these competitions to explore, re-think, and speculate on this fascinating architectural genre. They have presented a vast array of projects that demonstrate a truth and adherence to the discipline, while taking into account the above discussed considerations. They demonstrate a clear and at times masterful comprehension of the marked advances in technology and its implementation in environmental, structural, and formal issues.

We have identified three different design approaches used by the majority of the participants. The first one is a morphogenetic experimentation, using advanced CAD programs and parametric intelligent design to create "organisms" that evolve and grow according to program and context. Fields of data are transformed into virtually interconnected architectural forms that investigate dynamic relationships between structure, infrastructure, materials, users, and program.

The second one is a morphotectonic approach that through topological manipulation techniques, standard geometric units are shaped and transformed to give, structural, formal and programmatic solution to the skyscraper. The results could well be studied by a biology class as there are examples that resemble deep-sea sponges, honeycombs, ant colonies, and many others.

The third is a more conceptual approach which does not specifically answer a question, but puts forth a completely new theory about the future of the skyscraper. Inclusive in this group are projects that deal with not three, but seven potential dimensions of digital space-time and that look for ever changing spaces created by DNA controlled cells. Other projects still jump into the metaphysical terrain with utopian designs concerned more with explaining the nature of their reality instead of giving a specific skyscraper solution.

The past three years at eVolo have been an intensely fascinating, rewarding experience. We have been inspired and stimulated by the participants and would like to express our overwhelming gratitude for their hard work, talent, innovation and dedication. We would also like to express our gratitude to the architects that have served as tireless jurors for these competitions: Ada Tolla, Giuseppe Lignano, Alisa Andrasek, Fernando Velasco, Franklin Lee, and Evan Douglis. Finally, we would like to acknowledge winners of the 06 Skyscraper Competition: Changhak Choi, Gonzalo Pardo, Neri Oxman, José Muñoz-Villers, Yi Cheng Pan, and Mitchell Joachim who were jurors for the subsequent competitions.

A Lofty Index
The Skyscraper in the Age of the Digital Revolution

Neri Oxman

"What is the chief characteristic of the tall office building? It is lofty. It must be tall. The force and power of altitude must be in it, the glory and pride of exaltation must be in it. It must be every inch a proud and soaring thing, rising in sheer exaltation that from bottom to top it is a unit without a single dissenting line."
—Louis Sullivan's The Tall Office Building Artistically Considered (1896)

If there is one feature which characterizes the Modernist project in the twentieth century it is the skyscraper. In its vast scale and immensity the skyscraper has, by spirit and tradition, testified to the edge of design knowledge: in merging the idioms of architecture, engineering and technology, it has far exceeded any recognized typology in its cultural significance and impact upon design discourse in modern times. Since its invention during the 1880's, and triggered by the industrial revolution, engineers began experimenting with iron and steel, architects have explored the vertical curtain wall, and historians have marked the evolution of a new type. The skyscraper had it all: loftiness infused with market value, exuberance with engineering genius, urban ideals combined with place making. Modern masters owe their life to it, and for the Beaux-Arts avant garde, it was the raison d'être that brought down classicism. All in all, the skyscraper alone preserves the narratives of modern cultural and technological production. However, where there is novelty – there is crisis. And it is here to stay for the 21st century for as long as we grant it authority.

The skyscraper's architectural features, its urban presence, and the technological challenges it had presented to a generation of builders, have all contributed to the consideration of its value as iconic. Cities such as Beijing and Dubai are designed today in a manner which promotes their towers as a gateway for a thriving economy; construction workers are hitting new grounds in the Far and Middle East with a tower-per-day mentality; and global leaders consider it as the enabling mechanism for the establishment of identity. Since its origination, the skyscraper has served as an obelisk of the Modern movement. As a result, it has never transcended its value as an architectural, and indeed, an urban icon. In this light, the skyscraper has been traditionally associated with the image of the new as opposed to its functional expressions; It has abused the environment in prioritizing monumentality over responsiveness and adaptation; it has claimed to move forward technological innovation while regarding it as no more than an agency of production; in its repetitive nature, and homogeneity, it has valued structural and programmatic redundancy over efficiency and repetition over difference. It is nothing but sustainable and considering our earthy carbon footprint, it is nothing but the noble lofty. How may we overcome the syndrome of the obelisk?

Some have tried before us. In his Delirious New York Koolhaas proposes the contamination of program with mixed use by introducing unexpected functions juxtaposed with other programs. However editing functions and human activities was not always productive. There was an urgency to go beyond program.

A new generation of digerati architect and designers is now attempting to overcome the skyscraper's iconic crisis. They constitute a new avant-garde of design and are the cutting edge of contemporary architectural theory. Furthermore, occupying the boundary between theory, technology and practice, these digital designers/researchers are now advancing the theoretical frontier of design at the speed of technological development. Supported by elaborate 3-D environments promoting the generation of form and combined with state-of-the-art digital fabrication technologies, we are now facing the Difficult Tall (to paraphrase Venturi's search for architectural unity while promoting complexity and embracing contradiction). Our tools are bigger, faster and more efficient than ever. With them we can analyze, optimize, regenerate and evaluate a range of structural, environmental, and indeed social patterns of and for habitation. Adhering to a paradigm promoting difference and heterogeneity, where local control and behavior is made possible, we can now move forward from the icon to the index.

In Pierce's own words and followed by a generation of post-structural linguistics, the iconic stands in complete contradiction to the indexical. While the icon may be defined as an image that physically represents what it stands for, an index is defined by sensory features. The icon mimics or gives attribution to a singularity by way of contracting meaning through image; the index correlates with that singularity by mapping it relative to a given function. To demonstrate, the iconic form of a skyscraper withstanding north-west wind loads would be that of a twisted pyramid perhaps along with its monumental implications and random meanings; at the same time, its indexical representation would map every formal feature to the given vertical index of wind loads as analyzed and charted by the designer. More specifically, by employing dynamic spatial arrangements against the traditional organization of core and space, now made possible by digital media, we may dissolve the dichotomy between building and city, circulation and habitation, structure and skin, and other binary axioms in tall building design. These methods propose spatial layouts that establish heterogeneous movement, and not just assorted practices, as the criteria for a dynamic assemblage.

The distinction in design approach enables us to incorporate environmental, structural, social and urban conditions as lofty indexes informing the distribution of matter across its height. The implications are vast: the canonical floor space may be modified to enhance the absorption of light, relative to the building's orientation; The circulatory system – the elevator – so endemic to the type, may be treated as an entity which introduces sectional difference within the building; Structural load may potentially inform the interaction between load bearing components and skin features to result in a multitude of material organizations locally informed by weight and weather; and finally, environmental control could be made more efficient when allowing for natural ventilation to occur where possible.

Combined programmatic, urban, environmental, and technological aspects of designing, building and living tall – are now promoting a new paradigm that may permanently alter the modern vertical canon.

eVolo

06 SKYSCRAPER COMPETITION

Changhak Choi
United States

Even though we have reached an era of advanced technology, the majority of the skyscrapers are structures that don't provide sustainability to their social, cultural, and ecological environment.

In a contemporary and diverse metropolis, such as New York City, the skyscraper should be a reciprocal organism that interacts with its many different layers. In this case, the proposed skyscraper recognizes New York as a temporal residence for millions of students, artists, and tourists.

The proposed scheme analyzes their short-term needs and creates a system of organization around a single geometric unit. The combination of multiple units provides a structural, programmatic, and formal solution to the skyscraper.

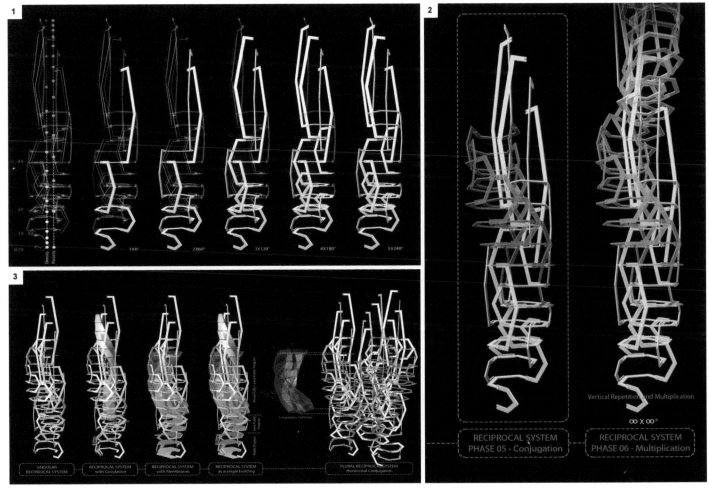

1 Open-end system
2 Reciprocal system
3 Systems combination

The proposed algorithm identifies the singularity and plurality of the geometric unit, depending on the location and use of the tower; a reciprocal system that adapts to its environment. The basic shape of this cell is a deformed hexagon that through multiplication, repetition, and deformation creates an open-end and close-end system.

Once a linkage technique between the units is established it is possible to explore a suitable reciprocal system for a specific location. A unit generates a basic open-end system by repeating, multiplying, and scaling. It grows upwards and downwards from the center allowing porosity and different programmatic events.

The system is complete only when every single requirement is met.

1

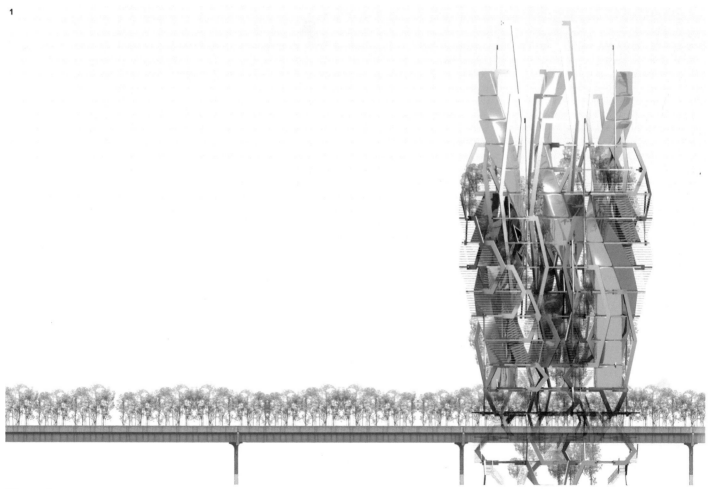

1 Cross section

>CONTINUOUS VERTICAL CITY

Gonzalo Pardo, Susana Velasco
Victoria González
Spain

When you visit Manhattan as a tourist you keep the city in your memory as a series of fragments, bodies, perceptions, sounds, and atmospheres. The position of everything is engraved in your memory; a new psycho-geographic map of the city is born.

We have chosen seven fragments of Manhattan, (5th Avenue, Broadway, piers, Financial District, Brooklyn Bridge, and Central Park), that could be thought about as individual cities; autonomous bodies, landscapes, and infrastructures.

With the use of manipulating and folding mechanisms we look for overlaps that cause hybrid conditions and programmatic impurities. The result is a tapestry of accidents engineered by our memory.

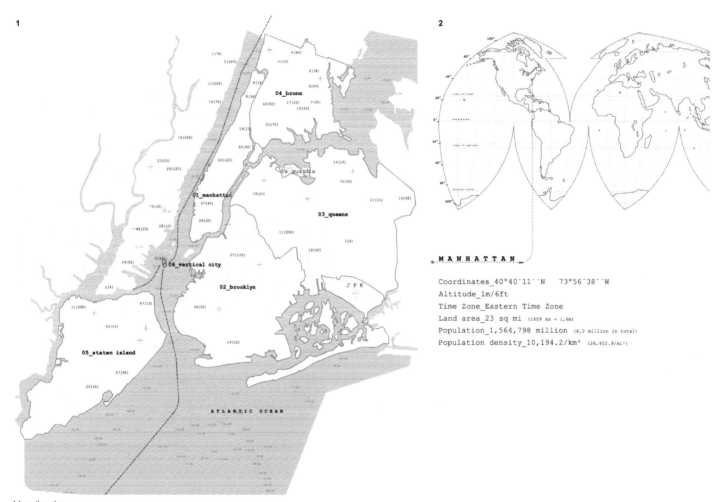

MANHATTAN

Coordinates_40°40´11´´N   73°56´38´´W
Altitude_1m/6ft
Time Zone_Eastern Time Zone
Land area_23 sq mi (1609 km = 1,6m)
Population_1,564,798 million (8,2 million in total)
Population density_10,194.2/km² (26,402.9/mi²)

1 Location plan
2 World location

When the defined fragments are folded into loops, a new city (skyscraper) full of intersections and possibilities emerges; a vertical three dimensional network. Instead of a conventional pile of floors, each level and section connect with different programs and situations in the upper and lower areas. In that way, all planes could be connected at least by one trajectory. The pile of folded surfaces would create a complex landscape, where program, circulation, and structure are one.

A skyscraper as an intensified vertical landscape emerges.

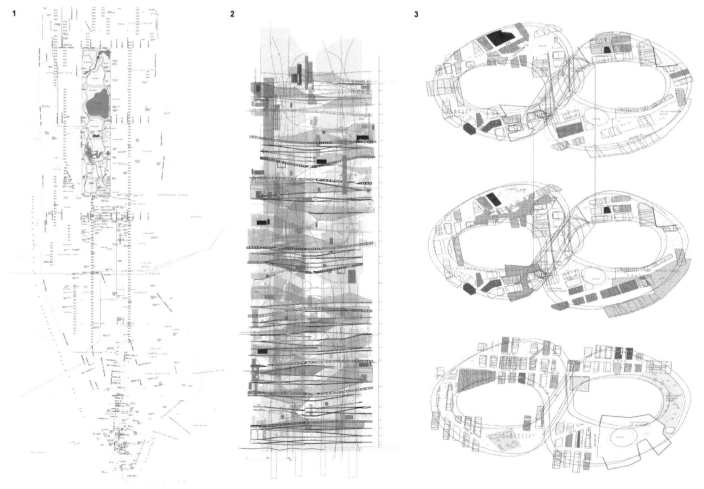

1 Psycho-geographic plan
2 Cross section
3 Plans

Peristalsis: The rippling motion of muscles in tubular organs characterized by the alternate contraction and relaxation of the muscles that propel the contents onward.

The core of the skyscraper, its structural and circulatory conventions, as a central obstacle to tall building design is well known. Should the elevator, of all things, persist as the non-negotiable limit of our vertical habitats? The limit is vexing, for not only does it determine compositional forms but, more significantly, the arrangement of social practices with regards to both our labor and leisure. Elevators stifle more than facilitate our movement by virtue of their rigid planes and fleeting occupations. That is to say, the vast space which the elevator shaft occupies is, temporally speaking, useless. But suppose we involved ourselves with a different interpretation of that inactive, rigid, and sequestered domain which much of this central shaft represents. It would demand a vital shift, or at least a conceptual reworking, towards an active utilization of such space.

By employing a dynamic spatial application against the traditional organization of core and space, we dissolved the dichotomy between circulation and habitable environments. We have eliminated typological stacking where experiences are vapidly suggested to be diversified by simply designating floors to particular social practices.

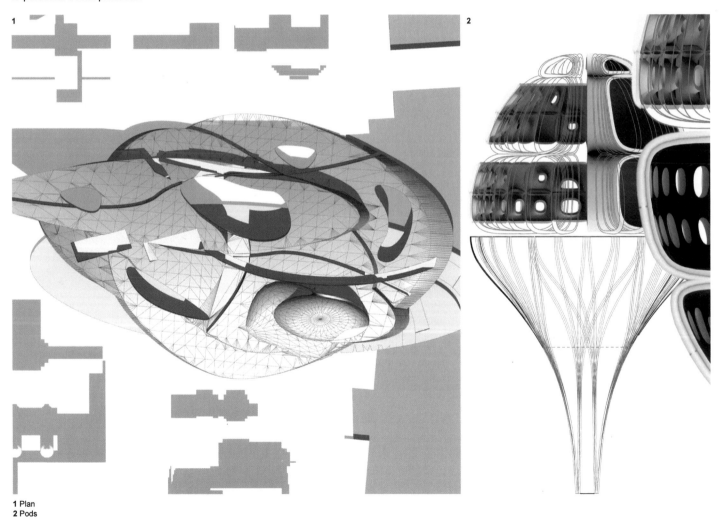

1 Plan
2 Pods

Ideation: Circulation = Space. An inhabitable pocket is contained within a flexible element. It is a module that flows in a vertical communicative field with the surrounding members. Their positioning is determined and managed by a responsive signaling system.

Technology: Fluidic Muscle Tectonics. This is a soft, pliable, sealed, and non-mechanical innovation which encapsulates the volumetric structure. Textile reinforced hoses execute a peristaltic action. Thus, the modules are enabled to create an articulated motion that is symbiotically connected to an urban armature.

Environment: Sky-Surface as Community Realm. The sky-surface is the eventual destination for the transportable unit occupants to celebrate with pleasured retreats and striking vistas overlooking the Hudson.

Perspective: Urban Window. The peristaltic-fabric is designed as a sequential organization around an 'urban window' condition; a visual gateway to both city and waterfront allowing a selection of interchanging viewing angles and heights. This temporal effect re-reads the city constantly, promoting a quality of transparency in the context of urban mass.

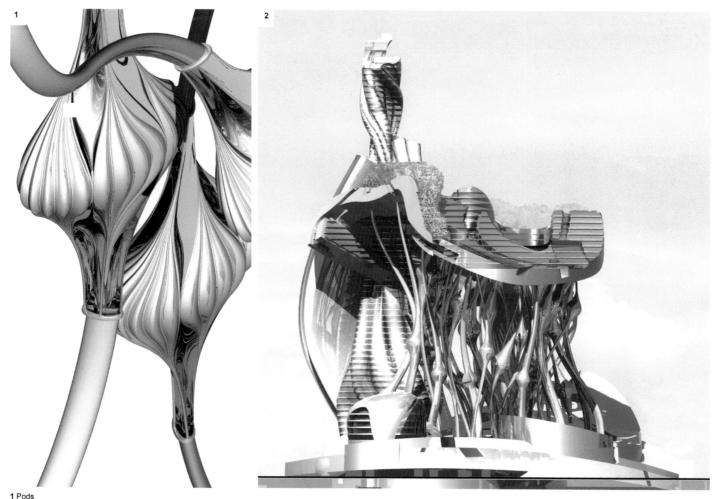

1 Pods
2 Perspective

>SKYSCRAPER FOR THE XXI CENTURY

Michael Samula
United States

Questioning what possibly is or will be the skyscraper for the XXI Century... It must not be singularly definable, but instead, in a multiplicious manner. A skyscraper for the XXI Century should act and react within itself as well as its context: both locally and globally, reconsider program and activity, generate new appetites, question standard fabrication techniques, create abundant spatial possibilities, and most of all, it must aim to redefine social identity and cultural conditions.

For instance, the proposal reacts to the forthcoming of an international train station aiming to decentralize Rome. The physical and cultural implications of such a project are immense, and the question is: how does a city prepare for such an abrupt change in its current fabric so that it will fully utilize this new transportation asset and flourish? In this case, it reaches out to international organizations and aspiring companies to become a hub in its international context. With an objective to facilitate conception and development of small seed companies, it strives to standardize procedures, strengthen Italy in Europe's existing biomedical field, and utilize local resources. By involving local resources, including but not limited to universities, hospitals, medical schools, businesses, and retailers; the skyscraper assists in generating an enduring presence within its local fabric, but more importantly connect itself and immediate context to international bodies. Within itself, it acts and reacts through a program proposal to standardize procedures.

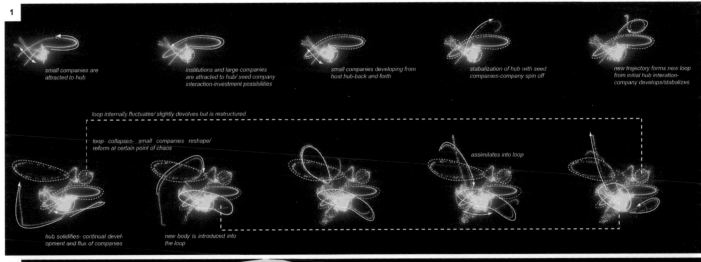

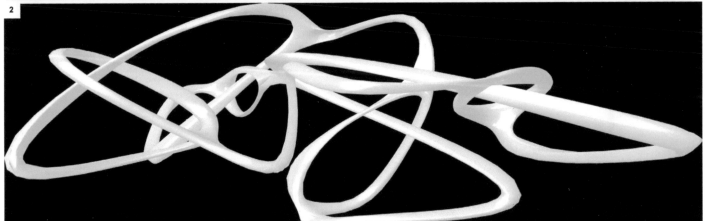

1 System analysis
2 Building block

Programmatically, the tower establishes a feedback loop. Initiating this is its connection with international bio-facilities to standardize procedures. By introducing these procedures and opportunities to small rising companies, acting as a host, companies grow; which later will affect the hub's procedural training and influence future small companies as well as those bodies that are internationally connected. Spatially, as a company develops, more facilities are available for their development. Within the tower, spatial possibilities provide for varying laboratories, freezer areas, lab support, holding rooms, and sample storage. All of which are possible through an open infrastructure.

The infrastructure was developed thanks to an understanding of a dynamic system. Its behavior-influenced conception is that of an abstract machine that allows multiplicious spatial possibilities. This infrastructure questions not only current fabrication techniques, but also spatial configurations. It redefines what wall, floor, structure, and enclosure are. Such a framework enables opportunities for different activities. As space develops, it affects the development of other spaces, when voids are full; each one can attract or repel growth of another. With spatial opportunity and new structural consideration, the sky-scraper of the XXI Century must do much more. It must redefine social identity and cultural conditions, and not conform to them. Looking at the proposal, one might argue that such an intervention seems out of place, out of scale, and inappropriate. On the contrary, it is exactly what the skyscraper should be. It must break conformity and redefine its environment as well as the cultural identity of its immediate community.

1 Perspective

Historically loaded and about to be demolished, the centrally located Hotel Rossija constitutes an exemplary terrain for an architectural operation. Starting with Lissitzky's Wolkenbügeln in the 1920's, followed by Stalin's 7 Sisters, and the Palace of the Soviets in the 1940's, there is a long history of skyscrapers in the city of Moscow. Contrary to planning of the new suburban business district "Moscow City", we propose our building to be located in the heart of Moscow.

Due to the lack of space a vertical arrangement of the program must be proposed within the perimeter of the Hotel Rossija. Relationships and dependencies between the different capitals resulted in the vertical configuration of the programs. The stacking of entire program typologies (e.g. soccer stadium, office blocks) resemble a vertical city rather than a conventional high-rise building.

The intensity of programmatic interaction expresses itself in the different degrees of spatial connectivity. The more a program depends on its opposite the closer it moves towards it. Consequently, the two towers rise separately and clash according to the climaxes of interaction. Horizontal infrastructure layers are inserted at every clash node to distribute the inhabitants. These infrastructure nodes function as public spaces comparable to squares and streets in the traditional city.

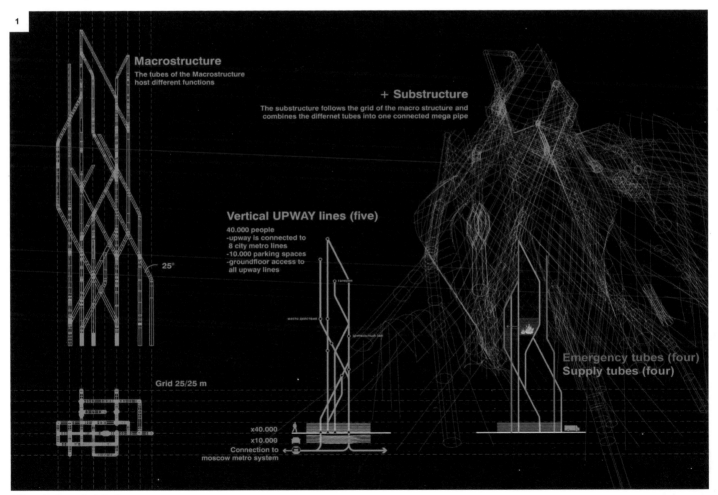

1 Macrostructure and substructure

The primary infrastructure system works on an urban scale to fulfil the needs of 40,000 people that circulate through the vertical city. Plugged into the Moscow Metro system the UP WAY opens a new district in the heart of Moscow. The UP WAY is able to run on the tracks of the Moscow subway system. They share the same gage of the track: 1520 mm (cabin diameter of connecting trains: 2,5 meters). For boarding and leaving, the cabins turn 90 degrees. UP WAY trains run with 3 cabins each, and transport 135 people, 45 passengers per cabin. Single cabins are connected by hinges. Several infrastructure layers function like node points from where the people are distributed through the programmatic clusters of the structure. The secondary infrastructure system compares to conventional high-rise circulation. The Macro-structure consists of a bundle of tubes within which the UP WAY is running.

By connecting the two towers, horizontal forces can become more efficient. The tubes are arranged in a 25m x 25m grid, then bend in one direction by 25°. They host different functions next to the UP WAY such as supply and emergency exits. Together with the substructure and the floor plates they form one Mega-tube.

1 Perspective
2 Moscow at night

Marco Vanucci
United Kingdom

In nature, organisms try to respond to the impact of various forces with minimum energy consumption. Similarly, materials are subject to a process of self-organization/adaptation in relation to the action of intrinsic as well as extrinsic forces acting upon it, aiming to fulfill a state of equilibrium. Exploring the inherent properties governing the behavior of a given material and its effects on the surrounding environment, represents the starting point for a broader understanding of material forms as a mutable, multi-performing, and generative design tool. The bottom-up approach towards the research onto a given material system discloses the opportunity to deeply investigate the proprieties of such a material, as well as opening unexpected potentials for inclusive performances and effects.

The aim of the research is to unfold a set of extensive investigations on catenary structures developing a generative tool-set for architectural design and overcoming the traditional notion of programmatic determinism and building types. The analysis of the properties of catenaries, the inherent relationship between geometry and structure, and the behavior of the material under the application of a set of experiments, represents the core of the research.

The hypothesis of the research is to develop an extensive set of investigations and trigger new speculations about the way catenary can nowadays be used, not only as global load bearing system to support vertical loads, but also as a geometry that can provide spatial arrangement for vertical structures. The parallel study on the physical and the digital realms constitutes the method of research.

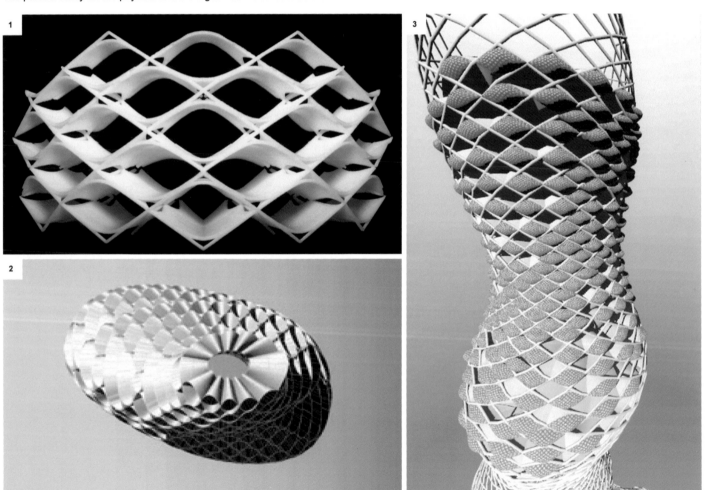

1 Facade detail model
2 Top view
3 Perspective

Understanding the built environment as a dynamic assemblage of generative material organization that yields potentials for inclusive performances represents, among other things, the starting point for a critical redefinition of building typology. Thus commonly considered as a rigid top-down organization within which every element plays a particular role and performs a specific task, the very idea of typology restricts the architectural discourse into codified standards where technology is the only driving force for innovation. Unfolding the organizational potential of high-rise buildings into a dynamic topological and morphological matrix where a multi-parametric material set-up opens up potentials and establishes a feedback loop between elements and their differentiation, shifts the discourse from typology to new ecology.

The Tsukiji fish market in Tokyo is the environmental testing ground where the system operates, modulating its morphology accordingly with external stimuli and internal organizational logics. The new high-rise building is integrated to the existing market representing its vertical extension. The existing market is characterized by a top-down layered organization whereby each element is aiming for a homogenous spatial standardization. The different degree of interiority within the building is achieved through an increasing number of material thresholds. The accumulation of discrete material sediments is defining the boundaries between different degrees of interiority-exteriority within the existing fabric. The new structure, instead, provides a differentiated generative system whereby local, regional, and global arrangements inform each other, defining new organizational distribution, as well as morphological, geometrical, and programmatic set ups.

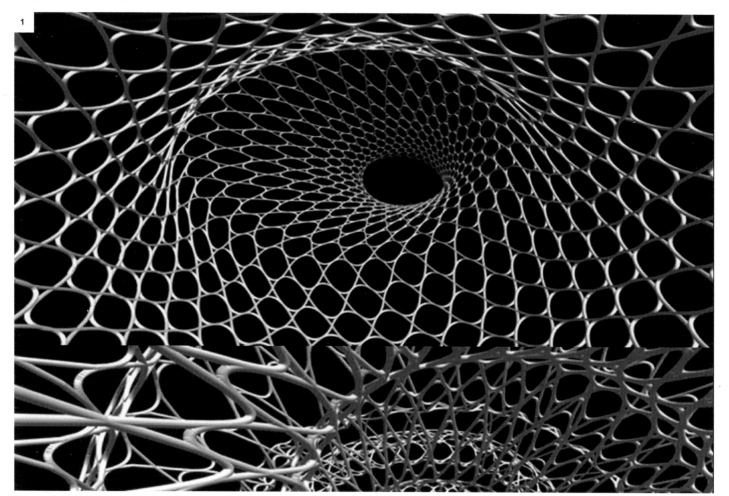

1 Structural system

>VENUS - BCN
Bioclimatic Vertical Sea Garden Skyscraper

Bea Goller
Spain

The site selected for the skyscraper is located on the Mediterranean Sea, off the Barcelona Waterfront, creating a grand vertical visual icon at the end of the Diagonal Avenue, in Barcelona; an urban axis, cutting the city grid on NE-SW angle, and finishing on the sea shore. It is erected on an artificial man-made peninsula, on which three intertwined towers would be built. They are entering a marine dominion, maybe representing utopia, extending the city, using a vertical element in a metropolis (Barcelona), while simultaneously turning toward the sky. It fulfills an old desired intention in an unconventional manner. We were inspired by deep-sea sponges to create a complex glass structure beneath the sea. We tried to apply our findings from this organism on a high-rise building, to create vertical marine structures, looking as garden towers, using a skin made of optical fiber and fiberglass. The three skyscrapers intend to be a new type of bioclimatic buildings, in total mimesis with natural organisms, inhabitants of the deep sea around them. The double skin is composed by two layers, and contains a third layer of suspended vegetation, which becomes a new type of urban vertical agriculture.

The Venus BCN skyscraper structures will also be ecological and energy self sufficient, having highly positive, repairing and productive results for the saturated urban environment, a sustainable design. For this reason, we propose an intelligent use of energy, water, and waste. This will be accomplished with a green bio-climatic envelope, which controls temperature, sun exposure, and ventilation, so the use of cooling and heating is kept to a minimum. The atmosphere water collector systems are implemented over the outer skin, and the use of bio-gas from the nearby purification plant would be implemented, having this as an energy resource, stored at the sky lobbies of each module.

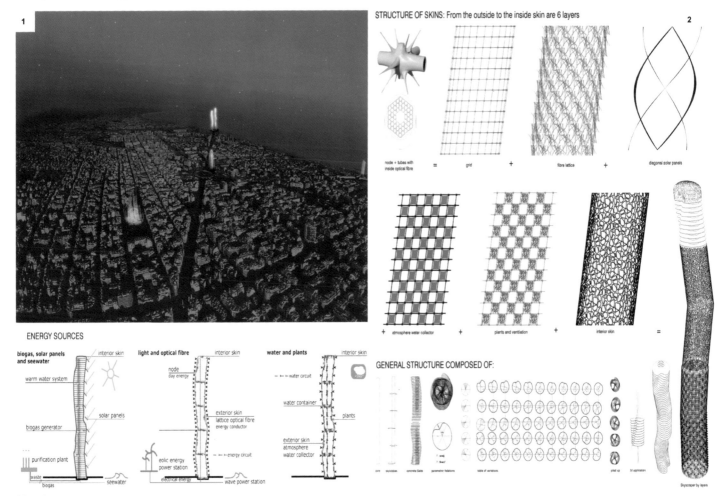

STRUCTURE OF SKINS: From the outside to the inside skin are 6 layers

1 Barcelona
2 Structure of skin

The outer skin structure will be made of fiberglass, as used in ships' construction, and other materials would be silica and optical fiber, with a steel core. The fibers that will comprise The Venus BCN skyscrapers' skeleton is composed by a lattice crisscross pattern. Its reinforcement would be made of fibers running diagonally in opposite directions, within alternating squares across the pattern. This construction technique will help counteract shear stress, which could easily cause a non-reinforced high-rise structure to collapse. The Venus BCN skyscrapers are divided in 6 segments on different slanted angles, which rotate themselves each at a 60, 120, and 180 degrees, in relationship to the gravity center. Each segment has a different use and remains as an independent element within the main structure. The joint between each of the segments is reinforced by a large open space, which doubles as a refuge zone, also housing energy management facilities, will serve as a Sky Lobby, as well. While the towers have different inclinations, only the elevator core remains as a central straight structure all the way to the top, a gravity center giving further structural stability to the towers. There will be 10 elevators in each of the cores, and four Sky Lobbies. At the end, we will have three shiny organic skins, which will emulate a live marine organism, varying from blue, purple to green tones, depending on the angle of the sun rays and varying with the seasons. It will glow at night, acting as a new type of lighthouse, which can be seen from approaching ships and planes. It will always change its colors, also depending on environmental conditions such as pollution or UV levels. The outside structure will act as a conductor of energy and information - due to the nature of fiberglass and optical fiber utilized of the outer skin, so the building will simultaneously be a receptacle and a conductor of electricity and telecommunication for its own use.

1 Aerial view
2 Interior garden
3 Interior and plans

>SKYFRAME
The vertical and horizontal skyscraper

Marco Steiner
Germany

How to transform horizontal into vertical?

The famous German architect Erich Mendelssohn once said: "Man can only find tranquility in today fast living in the motionless horizontal line".

How do we combine the vertical expression of the skyscraper with the serenity of a horizontal space? The "Skyframe" tries to answer this question. The Skyframe is a multifunctional skyscraper in which public areas such as conference center, shopping mall, cinemas, and recreational spaces are located on the ground floor. Restaurants and apartments are located in the upper part while the rising verticals allocate offices and meeting rooms. The vertical segments reflect the active and busy aspects of working life.

1 Barcelona Beach and skyframe
2 Skyframe at night
3 Public areas

The connectors between the verticals and horizontals are used as mechanical rooms for technical and energetic support. With a height and length of 500 meters, the Skyframe could be considered a very tall and massive building, but its unique design characteristics make it open and light.

The building is located in the Spanish metropolis of Barcelona, a city with one of the highest population densities in the entire world. The Skyframe is located by the sea, away from the busy downtown area and the surrounding mountains.

1

1 Piers

>SHANGHAI MARKET

Loren M. Supp
United States

Rather than looking at the city as an extension of architectonic space, the Shanghai market is here reinvented as an internal extension of a fluid landscape. Operating under this axiom, the vertical market changes the previous horizontality of the urban activity by pulling the city fabric upwards, enabling a further densification of the city.

While modeling the existing economic flows of the city there was revealed a potential for a systemic expansion of the streetscape skyward. This move enables an accretion of market functions, pulling the chaotic action to a single site. Formally and theoretically, the degradative nature of fluid market economics define the building architecture, the thickness of circulatory structure responds to the predicted expenditure of capital as one moves through the building, and space is allocated for market activity accordingly.

1

2

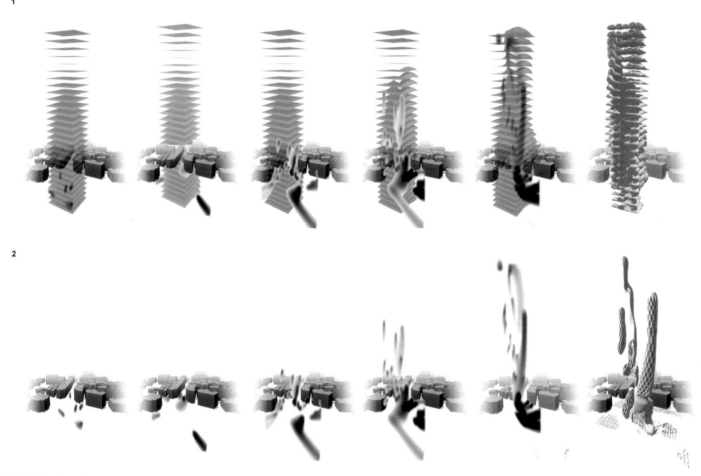

1 Building transformation
2 Urban forces

After initial studies into fluid tendencies of market vectors and their formal potentials, the spatial needs for a market were investigated using a dynamic technique reliant upon the structural generator of the fluid form, a typological skyscraper was deformed. The resultant change in topology was then used to define the spatial and formal conditions of the market itself.

The union of the fluid structure and its progeny allow for almost unlimited market program. Interconnected market spaces are united through a flowing structure and circulation, while the pods create an unlikely juxtaposition of both unity and definition. This juncture lies at the nexus of the Shanghai marketplace and citizenry, the need to blend in, to sell ,and to hide; or in the fluidic context of the city, to live and flow like the building that houses them.

1 Perspective
2 Aerial view
3 View from plaza

Marco Vermeulen, Theo Hauben
Netherlands

Although it is impossible to imagine contemporary life without car-based mobility, the car is frequently barred from the public space. In European inner cities, where pedestrians rule, the car is viewed as a threat to the city. This is rather strange because, in general, we spend a lot of money on cars and many car owners derive their social status from their possession, to a greater or lesser degree. In addition, sooner or later, most pedestrians become car users forced to descend into dark parking basements. Multi-storey parking facilities are an answer to the ever-growing demand for parking space, particularly where the concentration of activities requires the well-conceived use of space available.

The design is a 100 meter-high tower, with a capacity for approximately 450 cars, with an entry and exit station at the base of the building. This station has been designed with the users, both motorists and pedestrians, in mind. Spacious platforms for getting in and out and comfortable waiting rooms characterize the design.

1 Aerial view
2 Street view

The entry, transfer, and garaging of vehicles is automated and takes place behind the station. The horizontal transfer is carried out by a traverse robot, whereas the vehicles are transported vertically in the tower by six car lifts. By uncoupling the cycle of getting in and loading the car, transporting it and parking it and the reverse process, a high rate of arrivals and departures is achievable. In principle, nobody is allowed behind the platforms and this has many advantages regarding efficient space usage. This separation is also advantageous in terms of safety and security for both motorists and their cars. The tower is flanked by a fire-escape stairwell for technical maintenance purposes.

The limited space in the Delta metropolises (Rotterdam, The Hague, Amsterdam, and Utrecht) require compact parking facilities. The high groundwater level in this urban agglomeration makes underground construction highly expensive. The parking tower with its minimal footprint is the ideal solution. However, the parking tower is more than an efficient parking facility. The parking of cars on the skyline in quick tempo is a visible spectacle. The appearance of the tower changes constantly throughout the day depending on the number of cars parked. Whereas a full tower creates a colorful palette, at less busy times it will gain in transparency. With this visual spectacle, the facility evolves into an attraction and the city acquires an icon.

1 Entrance pavillion
2 Detail

>THE "A" COMPOSITION

Ratsimiebo Noely, Bommier Pacome
Bruter Jonathan
France

A new layer in the city

Let us think of a city that is constrained by a complex urban structure. An ordered grid, the compulsory maximal height and density of the imposed vellums, as well as the need for balanced perspectives and visual openings. Every new modification of the city must abide by a strict global composition. The city is also centralized, its urban layers are superimposed, add to each other, organize and stabilize disparities and dis-equilibria. The city can be seen as an ecosystem made of built components, equipments, infrastructures, sport fields, empty spaces, squares, parks, and gardens. The site and placement of each of them is conditioned by a global equilibrium which allows every single element to exist on its own, as well as within a global system. It is a balanced composition.

Now, let us think of this city as a finished ensemble, in which urban logic might be enriched by a new, unexpected, dimension. What if its current equilibrium is not complete, but, instead, a living body, which could be enriched and even improved by the addition of a new dimension? What if this new dimension is a vibration that would allow the whole city to live and function differently?. New levels of connection, new links within a city, a city that did not think it had any room for them. This role would by played by high buildings, which would inject a density of life in areas that were thought to be complete: in-between a courtyard and a street, amidst towers and offices, topping an empty tooth, to give a meaning to a district that used to lack it.

1

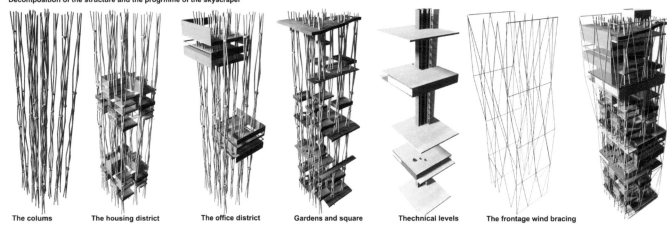

2

Decomposition of the structure and the progrmme of the skyscraper

| The colums | The housing district | The office district | Gardens and square | Thechnical levels | The frontage wind bracing |

1 Potential locations
2 Components

Functioning of the towers

Each tower is conceived as a new complex object. Rich in links, connections, public and private spaces, they are thought of as jigsaws of habitation spaces, working quarters, and areas of life and human interaction. Each element finds its place in a network of pillars and develops its own specific architectural vocabulary. The apartments are inserted like cabins on groups of pillars. The habitation areas spread over a height of 17 metres. Within the volume of the building, plateaus of 5.25m x 7.60m are superimposed, creating duplex and triplex apartments as well as aerial gardens. This mixture of lodgings, gardens, and axes of circulation create a complex system of public and private spaces, full and empty elements, where transparencies open, focus, and direct the views within the tower and to the outside.

Perched high, apartments are linked by open air corridors, 'cursives' and ramps, which reach several points in the volume of the building via platforms of distribution. Office blocks are hubs within the vertical structure of the tower. They are surrounded by technical floors and come as overhanging structures, creating breaks in the organization of the building. These blocks are made of five plateaus of about 350 square metres. These stages can be separated, open, or broken in smaller parts depending on the space needs of the companies that will use them. This means that a company that needs two or more levels can open an underpass or mezzanine to fulfil their needs. The overhanging structures of these boxes create empty spaces within the pillars, which serve as common spaces for the surrounding offices.

1

2

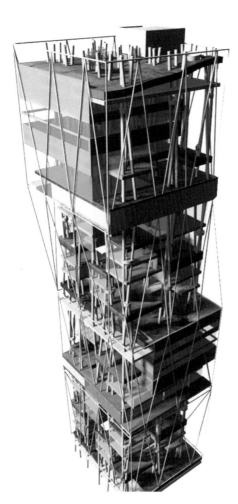

Roof public space

Offices district

Technical level

Housing district

Public space, supermarket

Offices district

Public space, Restaurant

Housing district

Public space, Libary

1 Elevation
2 Program diagram

>RE-DESIGNING HONG KONG

Justyna Karakiewicz, Jeff Cheng,
John Kao
Hong Kong

Hong Kong is a city of extreme landscape conditions in which the majority of the land is defined as high steep terrain. Due to this condition there is a complex infrastructure of trains and escalators for the mobility of the pedestrians. This type of infrastructure accounts for more than 50 percent of the available land. The remaining areas are clustered with isolated skyscrapers surrounded by heavy vehicular and pedestrian traffic.

Because of this phenomenon, we think that Hong Kong doesn't need another skyscraper but a building that will offer public areas for the inhabitants. Causeway Bay, one of the most heavily populated areas in the world, is defined by a large public park to the east and a major traffic route to the north. An entrance to the Cross Harbor tunnel is also located in this area. Slow moving traffic is a constant all-day long, causing intense noise and pollution. The traffic spreads to the surrounding streets and heavily suffocates the neighborhood. The only access to the harbor front is through a pedestrian tunnel, which was originally built as water infrastructure. This has lead to a deserted waterfront with a lot of residual spaces. By identifying this land we come up with an interesting development proposal that would provide a large number of public areas, as well as housing and office spaces. This proposal is designed in phases and will grow through the years. It will also regenerate the harbor and will bring back life to this area of Hong Kong.

1

2

1 Plan
2 Elevation

1

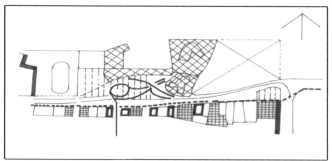

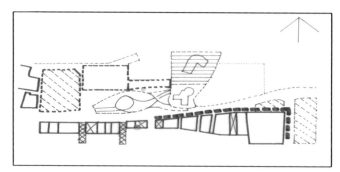

2

3

1 Land use analysis
2 Site plan
3 Longitudinal section

Adelaide Marchi, Nicola Marchi
France

In their search for light, space, balance, and keeping up with the environmental forces, trees are their own architects. A tree's shape is a fascinating question. One part of its development is generated by its genetic code and the other part by its adaptation to the environment. We think these two factors are the key to understanding architectural design.

Hong Kong is built next to the China Sea; viewed from the open sea, skyscrapers resemble the edge of a forest. In high-density areas, skyscrapers act like a forest, where buildings compete for light and space. The dynamism of the forest originates in the chemical exchanges with the ground, while that of the city derives from the interaction of economic and demographic forces. Paradoxically, trees which are the major structures in nature, can become dwarfed in an urban setting. The aim of this project is to return trees to their central role, in the way they dominate the natural environment.

Like a tree, this building aims to be self-sufficient. It produces its own energy using sun and wind power. The tower is designed according to the principles of sustainability in terms of both its shape and its use of materials and renewable energy. The quasi-cylindrical shape offers less wind resistance and the circular floors are radially shifted in six different positions to allow better lighting at each level.

1 Plan, facade
2 Plans, aerial view

The building is designed based on the construction principles used in oil rigs, namely a primary structure composed of three large pillars supporting circular floors (66m in diameter), open in the middle to incorporate multiple spatial modules with various functions. The first floor rises 40 meters above the ground, freeing up a large amount of space and giving access to the street. Accordingly, the lobby is located in the basement along the parking and it is naturally lit from the top by a system of circular skylights.

The three main structures contain elevators and emergency staircases which are wider in the lower part of the tower. These structures will be made of a combination of metal and concrete in order to allow greater transparency. In addition, the partly glazed elevators will allow viewing to the interior and exterior.

The tower is virtually self-sufficient in terms of electricity required for lighting, domestic use, and office equipment, as well as for an interior regulating climatic system. Some of the required energy is produced by solar modules placed on the facade. The central atrium acts as a chimney in which air ascends due to the natural draft generated by the pressure difference between the base and the summit. The air currents in the central well are used to propel turbines located in the summit.

1

2

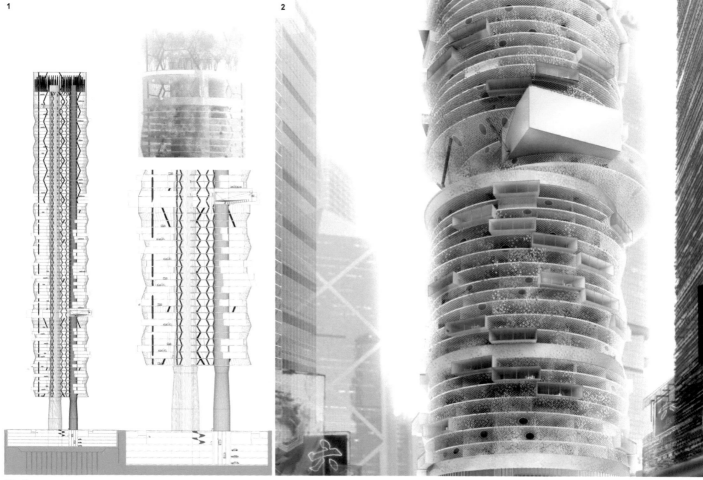

1 Sections
2 Street view

>THE GENOTOWER 05

Nicholas Pisca
United States

The Genotower05 was an investigation of the potential of 7+ dimensional digital space-time, established through an ever-changing search space which uses a stratification of sculpted numeric and geometric randomness in a resonant eugenic single-celled generative automaton. This stem-cell recursively duplicates, splits and mutates under multi-dimensional distortion. While self-mutilating to isolate regional topological growth, it eventually sheds aged generational cells and produces individualized but intelligent organs, situated in an overall organic structure on multiple transgenic levels. In other words, it was to grow intelligent vertically oriented organs in an intelligent transgenic body from identical digital stem cells, without linear array sets or post-processing.

When dealing with the antiquated topological organ assembly, which may be laterally-transgenic and operating to develop mutation on different affective and performative levels, it remains still a tapeworm, missing core elements of an architectonic assembly. This assembly establishes skin, interior conditions, and nascent organ development individualization, but it remains confined to the longitudinal direction prescribed in the geometry or number set. There is little opportunity to describe clear organ isolation nor to establish formal splitting and return, without disrupting the skin/scale membrane or interior network structure. The Genotower05 does not operate in this confined linear topological fashion. It grows, lives and dies from a cell that recursively develops in many directions to construct a body of living cells communicating with each other.

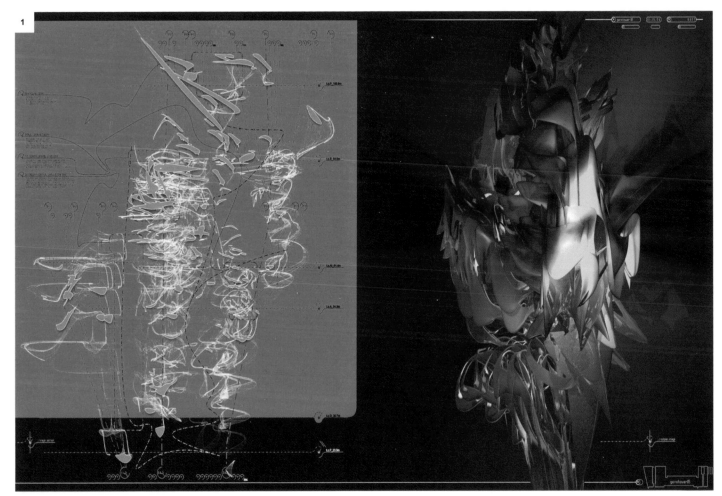

1 Section, elevation

These systems were infused with the individual cellular locomotion, at first randomly, to allow for multi-celled formal arrangements. To better isolate future "heart" or "lung" or "nerve" cells, the initial stem-cell's locomotion is allowed extreme degrees of freedom. As each generation progresses, the intermediate vector becomes more localized so that the cells remain near their cousins and siblings, not to cause intermingling of individual organs. Viewers should understand that this research is not trying to use a breeding algorithm to create complexity in a system that is actually asexual. There is no multi-partner reproduction and nor would this be plausible construct when dealing with zygotes. This process is not devising a speciation of organisms, but more contributing to a body through the individualization of organs but still assemble the whole on two+ scales of assembly.

During the research on the Genotower05, the Lo-III process became instilled with a global mutator. Similar to control DNA broadcasting chemical instructions to "unspecified" cell-types, this global modifier alters the children's form subtly so that it is apparent that it is a descendent of the parent, but different. After defined generational development, organs emerge from "de-unspecializing" clusters as the deceased elements are projected into the vertical direction, in an operation comparable to how a nautilus fabricates a spiral shell. To instruct the cells to have a more intelligent mode of differentiation, one needs two types of mutation, global and regional. The "rand[$x]" work demonstrated how a single organ could maintain transgenic behavior from similar or identical lateral constructs, as long as the regional mutator was programmed to affect their form accordingly.

1 Street view

Guillem Augé, Anna Vergés
Spain

The skyscraper for the XXI Century must respond to 100 years of evolution in technology and society. New materials and structures allow the construction of buildings which are 700 to 900 meters high. More research will allow rising up to 1200 meters. The skyscrapers are moving from the old North American or European cities to the new Asian and South American cities. They used to be constructed in the city's downtown, but are changing to the suburbs, with the intention of revitalizing them.

In the past, they used to be offices in high-density financial districts, such as Manhattan, London, and Hong Kong. Now, skyscrapers have multifunctional spaces for commercial, living, and working activities.

The detached single family house, the "spam", has infected the earth as a virus, and if we apply this model to the rest of the world, with its actual growth of population, the Earth will soon be over urbanized. Europe and the United States export their image of the family, the house, the garden, the car and the dog, but it has been proven that this model generates insecurity, environmental problems and is not "sustainable" for all. In the third world countries, the "fabelas" are also common around the urban centers, extending over the territory like the "single family house" model.

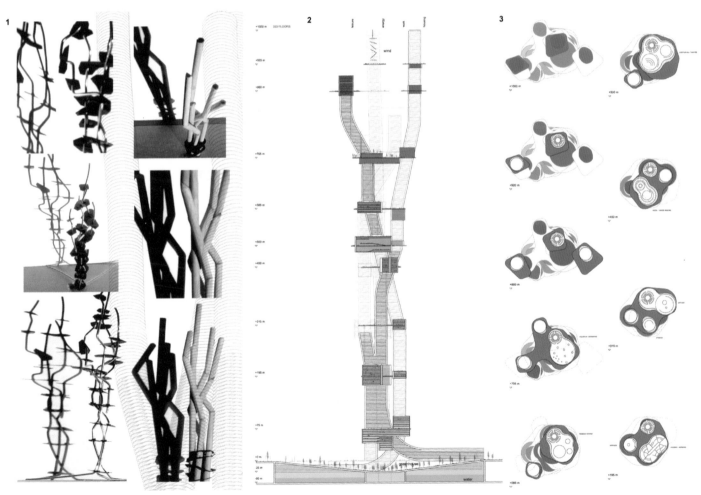

1 Concept diagrams
2 Cross section
3 Plans

This project is not a single building, but a group of buildings that resemble the branches of a tree. At one point the building adds more than 1.000.000 sqm of space, with an implantation of just 2500 sqm. It will be located in suburban areas, which will benefit from its multiple services and amenities. This skyscraper could be constructed using the same variables around the world as a strategic solution, but will change in each place depending on the climate, density, and development of the city.

The basement floor adapts its shape and height to the existing buildings. It has a big greenhouse with trees and plants, which rise the temperature of the air between opposite extremes to create currents that move turbines. We also have a water container for the recycling of the rainwater, also used to control the building's climate.

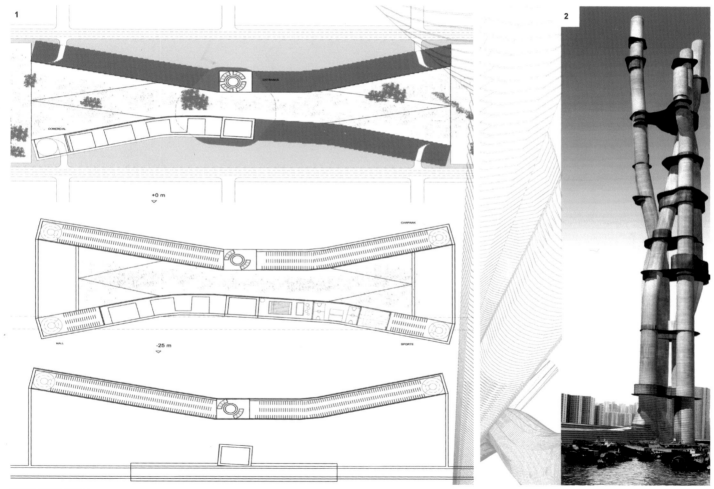

1 Ground plan, parking
2 Perspective

This skyscraper is designed as a vertical city. The structural grid is inspired by a city's master plan and its infrastructure system. The three cores are used to open up the whole building. The six planes are the horizontal connection between the cores.

The cores contain several public spaces like parks, gyms, and meeting rooms. Infrastructure, such as electricity, water, and weather control, is also supplied by the cores. The second part of the building are the pods. Their construction system is similar to cabins in shipbuilding. The primary cover includes all technical links without interior finish. The interior finish is done in a nearby "shipyard" based on the client's wishes. During the second phase, the module is carried to the skyscraper structural grid by building cranes. Water, electrical supply, and telecommunications are installed by "plug and play". The skeleton is filled up with modules in this way.

Modules could also be combined. It's possible to create apartments out of two or more modules by connecting them horizontally and/or vertically. Inhabitants that move out give the module back to the shipyard where the interior finish is removed. The cover is consequently prepared to be sold and refinished for a new inhabitant. Therefore the buildings skin is changing all the time and it is possible to react to clients wishes and technical progress in facade or design technology.

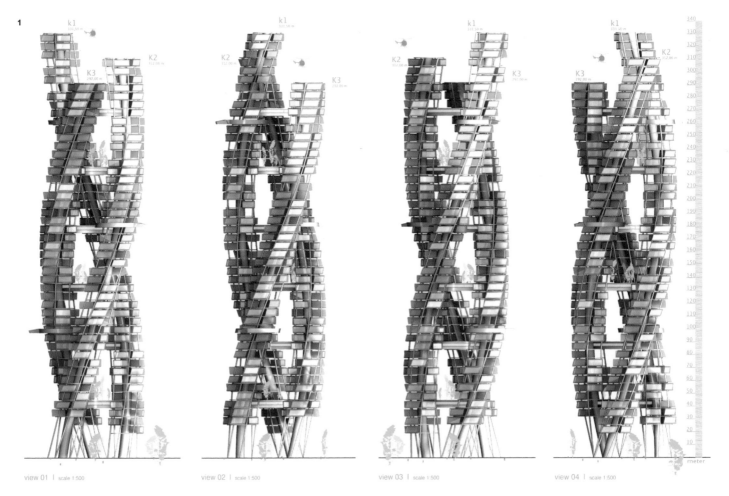

view 01 | scale 1:500   view 02 | scale 1:500   view 03 | scale 1:500   view 04 | scale 1:500

1 Elevations

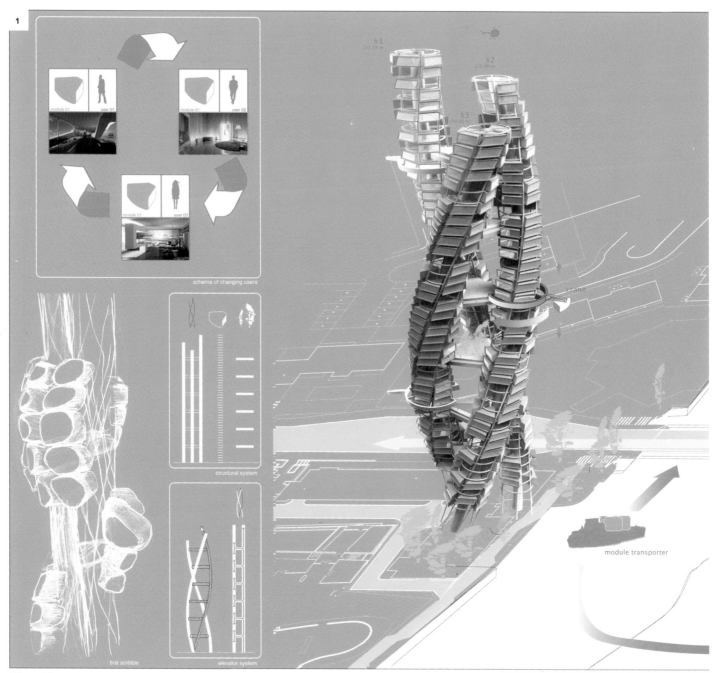

schema of changing users

structural system

first scribble

elevator system

1 Concept diagrams

>BILLBOARD SKYSCRAPER

Edwin Liu, Nathaly Der Boghosian,
Felix Monasakanian, Efren Soriano,
Hugo Ventura
United States

This project is an examination of the skyscraper typology being driven by financial and market forces. Reaching a maximum height of nearly 800 feet, the building performs as a revenue-generating billboard on an urban scale.

The envelope of the structure was generated to maximize advertising perception from key cultural and civic nodes throughout the surrounding context of the greater Los Angeles area. The invasive insertion of this massive entity into the downtown area alters or destroys existing sight lines and replaces them with corporately sponsored images. Living rent-free in the towering structure are residents that are participants in the performance of the building as advertising conduit.

The entity is composed of a swarm of pod-like enclosures, each creating a single pixel on the surface of the billboard. Essentially, this forms a giant low-res media surface. Each pod is terminated with a dome of electronic smart-glass that has the ability to change opacity and hue.

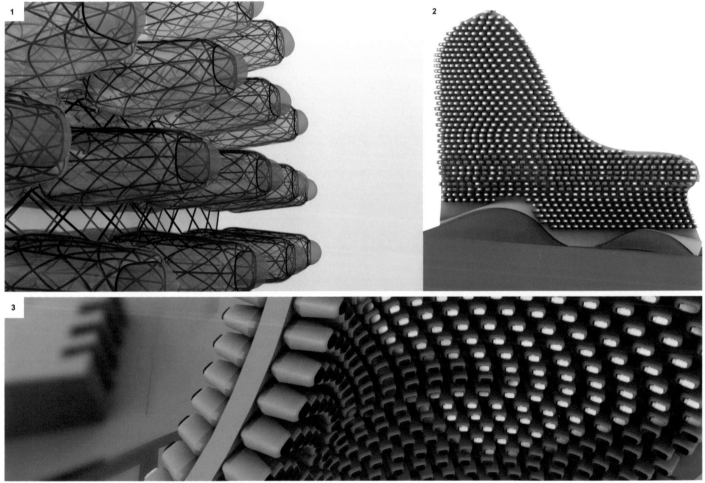

1 Pods detail
2 Elevation
3 Pods as billboard

The dome also functions as the inhabitant's only window out of the capsule. In coordination with RFID tags embedded in participating advertiser's products, sensors within each pod determine the level of consumer activity that an individual produces. In a typical scenario, consuming more of the 'correct' brand clears the window to full transparency, removing the 'pixel' as a participant in the advertising façade.

Consumer inactivity or consumption of the 'wrong' products causes the smart glass to become opaque. The machine operating at full commercial potential produces a surface punctuated by transparent windows, while a machine operating below established market criteria will compensate by activating the surface with advertising.

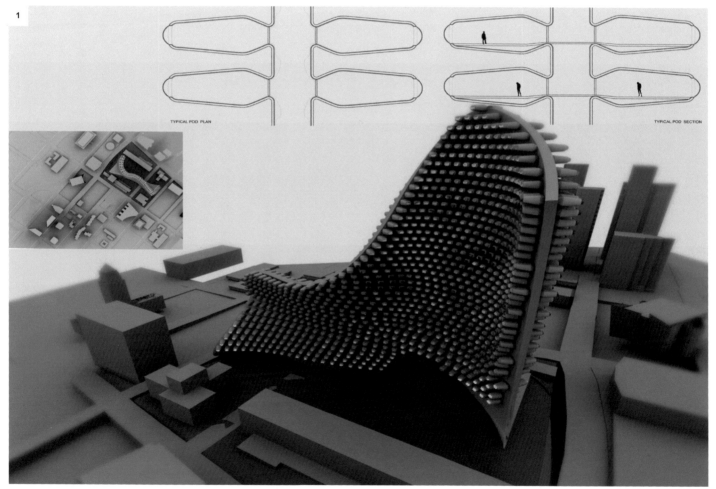

1

TYPICAL POD PLAN

TYPICAL POD SECTION

1 Section
2 Aerial view

Carrie Norman
United States

The main aim of this proposal is to question the role of structure within the field of architecture. Can it have multiple roles that integrate other elements, systems, creating mutually beneficial conditions? Can it be modeled like a leaf, in which the very members that hold it together are the same that deliver its nutrients? If so, structure can be a conduit—a physical network of rigid arteries and veins that not only bear load, but also house and perform additional services and operations. This scheme proposes that a research institute become a responsive, working system that utilizes structure and technology to yield agriculture, and effectively contribute to the efforts of reducing energy consumption that results in transporting fruits and vegetables from rural to urban areas. A canopy of hydroponic garden pods is designed to function as a seasonal market for the Philadelphia community.

The proposal can be dissected into three interconnected components: stem, core and roots. Structure becomes the overlapping connective tissue that integrates these. The stem is the prominent element in which the others organize. It acts as the water processor. The core becomes a protective wrapper around the stem, benefiting from its branches' deliveries of water. Collaborative lab space fills the core. Three currently independent research entities within the Pennsylvania region will merge like roots into one stem: urban horticulturalists, environmental scientists and those investigating building performance and diagnostics, will thrive from each others' efforts and passions concerning future environments. Finally, the roots transfer water back to the ground, completing the natural hydrologic cycle. This scheme assumes it can be constructed above an existing parking garage on 12th and Sansom Street, Philadelphia.

1

store

distribute

1 Street view

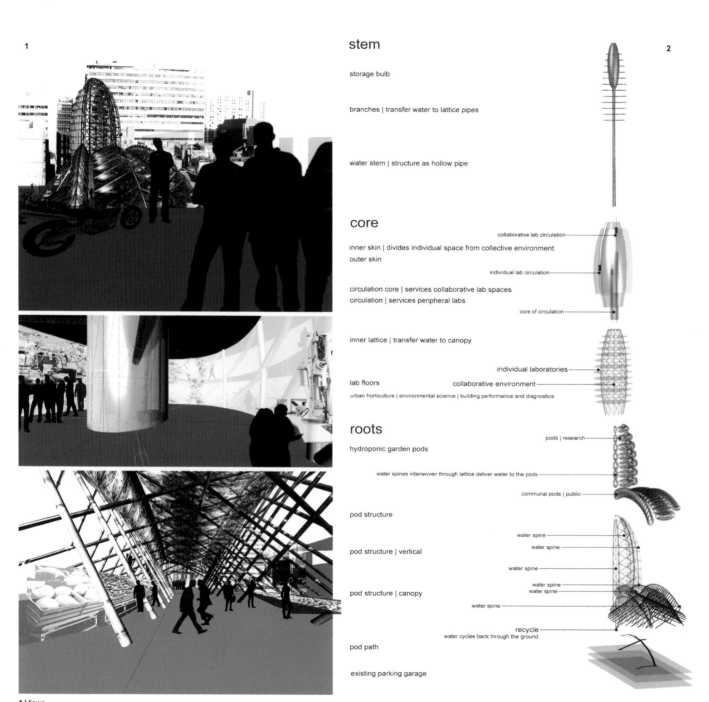

stem

storage bulb

branches | transfer water to lattice pipes

water stem | structure as hollow pipe

core

inner skin | divides individual space from collective environment
outer skin

circulation core | services collaborative lab spaces
circulation | services peripheral labs

inner lattice | transfer water to canopy

lab floors
urban horticulture | environmental science | building performance and diagnostics

collaborative lab circulation

individual lab circulation

core of circulation

individual laboratories
collaborative environment

roots

hydroponic garden pods

water spines interwoven through lattice deliver water to the pods

pod structure

pod structure | vertical

pod structure | canopy

pod path

existing parking garage

pods | research

communal pods | public

water spine
water spine
water spine
water spine
water spine
water spine

recycle
water cycles back through the ground

1 Views
2 Concept diagrams

>CHICAGO SKYSCRAPER

Kyle Schlie
United States

A skyscraper does not need to be about height, or technological achievement, but should firstly strive to provide healthy and diverse spaces for living and working. Density and vertical programming do not necessitate identical isolated units.

The new skyscraper is de-objectified to foster urban connectivity, green space, and community life. It looks not just to fit within the city, but to extend new fits to nearby buildings and public spaces. The building creates new street life in the existing dead space between Michigan Avenue and State Street. The program addresses Chicago's need for affordable housing. Failure to provide new housing as housing projects are being continually demolished is only increasing the number of people without suitable living arrangements.

The housing program includes transitional housing, SRO units, hostel rooms, and market-rate condominiums. Each floor has a variety of unit types. The housing program works by providing accompanying services like day care, job assistance, dog walking, food mart, parking, recycling center, community kitchen, and laundry within the building. The base of the building consists of street side retail, offices, restaurants, and grocery shops. Parking is pushed to the interior of the site and accessed from the basement by a ramp off Illinois St. A new roof above the Lake Shore Athletic Club is a public park.

1

1 Street view

The building itself is a means of individual expression and a source of pride among its occupants. Rather than showcasing a repetitive structure or curtain wall, the facade, through resident chosen paint and decoration schemes, expresses the differences that feed the vibrant city. Public space facades are determined by vote among members or users of the specific space. The skyscraper's traditional exterior is abandoned and it instead becomes a simple record of its interior. Resident controlled planting beds also promote ownership.

Shared artificial ground planes every third floor promote community activities and provide ample shared space, not typically found in skyscrapers. The three level housing blocks promote interactions among a smaller group of neighbors. Upper level parks and green spaces also promote collective activities. The Sun atriums are source points for heat storage and temperature controlled natural ventilation (stack and cross). Also functioning as greenhouses, residents can grow vegetables and flowers in these atriums. The three level U-shaped housing blocks lean toward the south to minimize the building shadow and to provide summer shade to the unit directly below. Rain water is collected from all horizontal surfaces and directed to cisterns for irrigation and laundromat use via the fire stair roof. The planted roof filters water as it winds down through the building.

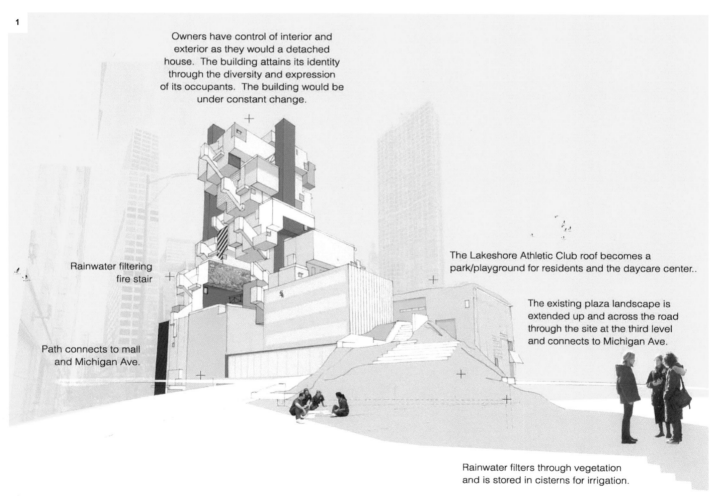

1

Owners have control of interior and exterior as they would a detached house. The building attains its identity through the diversity and expression of its occupants. The building would be under constant change.

Rainwater filtering fire stair

Path connects to mall and Michigan Ave.

The Lakeshore Athletic Club roof becomes a park/playground for residents and the daycare center..

The existing plaza landscape is extended up and across the road through the site at the third level and connects to Michigan Ave.

Rainwater filters through vegetation and is stored in cisterns for irrigation.

1 Concept diagram

>ONE-HALF INFINITY TOWER

Leonard Ng
United States

Originating from the Klein Bottle, a non-orientable mathematical surface, it is similar to a Mobius strip in that it is single-sided. Its potential for spatial application is where the Mobius strip falls short, for the Klein Bottle is fully 3-dimensional and flirts with bounding volume with an infinite, single continuous side. It can be perceived as a strange tube which, in an attempt to bend & form a normal torus/loop, self-intersects and rejoins with itself but on the wrong side. The key lies in its strange quality of self-intersection, for the self-intersection provides spatial, typological, programmatic, structural, technological, site, and sustainability opportunities.

It represents a new topological family of form, which can spawn a variety of skyscraper designs; the represented ½ Infinity Tower represents only one iteration of a family of architectural explorations. The ½ Infinity Tower provides a third spatial center/focus to the traditionally bipolar (top/bottom) skyscraper, for it creates a new void at the center third which can be programmed as a public or collective space: exhibition, meetings, restaurants, atrium, sky garden. The middle of the tower is, for once, a highly coveted destination within the skyscraper. The planimetric cut plane through the building is constantly evolving. Moving from a continuous floor plate to a two tower configuration, to a C-shaped floor, and finally a reconstituted single floor plate once again, the tower provides multiple shaped floor plates of varying sizes for companies of all sizes to occupy and inhabit. The increase in surface area not only allows for greater natural light and ventilation, but also much greater view opportunities, both outward-looking and inward-looking, at all areas of the skyscraper.

1

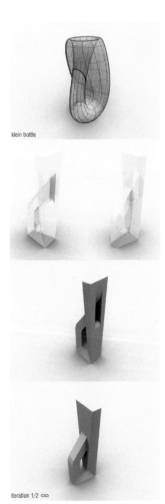

klein bottle

iteration 1/2 ∞

2

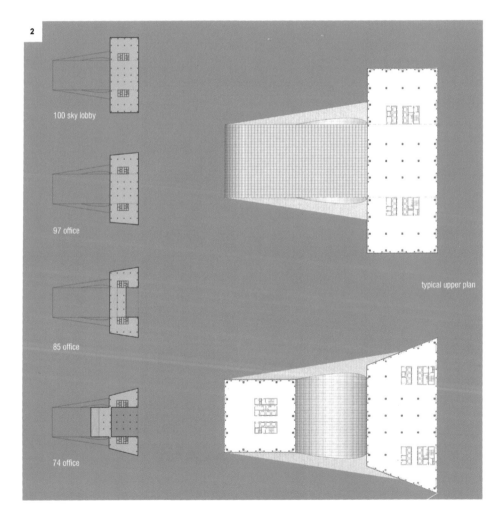

100 sky lobby

97 office

85 office

74 office

typical upper plan

1 Concept diagrams
2 Plans

The ½ Infinity Tower's self-intersecting form increases the lateral stiffness and stability of the skyscraper significantly. As most skyscrapers can be perceived as a cantilever from the ground plane with only one point of support, the self-intersection of the tower shortens the cantilever by half and provides an additional point of lateral support at the midpoint for the skyscraper. If one perceives the project as two towers that merge, then each tower effectively braces the other. The self-intersection/void at the center of the building has an opening at the top, allowing wind to pass through the building and reducing wind loading substantially. The gravity loads of the tower are taken up by the triple core and internal columns. A steel lattice, or diagrid, envelopes the entire structure, producing a very efficient and redundant means of resisting lateral load and reducing total tonnage of steel throughout the building, as opposed to a traditional moment-frame. Where the tower cants, transfer trusses two floors deep, coupled with the diagrid lattice, transferring forces back down the vertical towers and into the ground.

The self-intersection of the building is functional in myriad ways. As mentioned, it increases the overall structural performance of the building, provides a third programmatic/ spatial center to the skyscraper, increases natural light to the deep floor plates at the center, and allows for mechanical exhaust and natural ventilation through the stack effect for the office space. The self-intersection also allows multiple paths of exiting travel during an emergency (fire, typhoon, earthquake) and provides an exterior refuge floor for increased safety for its occupants.

1

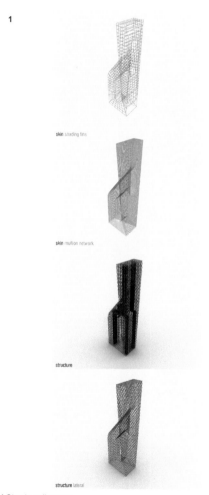

skin shading fins

skin mullion network

structure

structure lateral

2

1 Structure diagrams
2 Perspectives

eVolo

07 SKYSCRAPER COMPETITION

Somnath Ray
India

The skyscraper as a 'modernist' invention was a logical conclusion to the desires of a paleo-capitalist society, as an urban landmass approached its critical point of wealth and density of inhabitants. Imagined as a sign of cultural power and ownership, the skyscraper was typified in its 'classical heroism' from its logically consequent *tabula rasa* condition; as a formulation for a utopian blank slate on which a new building is conceived, free of compromise or complication after the demolition of what previously stood on the site.

Any speculation to the order of formulating a 'new' condition of the 'skyscraper' must encounter this semantic intent and deviate from its historical tendencies. Contemporary speculations on the typology of the skyscraper side-step the essential semantic dimension and instead, merely engage with a technological evolution of its species (intelligent systems, efficient circulation, stronger structure, energy efficiency, environmental consciousness etc.). Although some radical formulations of the mega-structures, such as Archigram, Constant and the Metabolists, as designs of pure infrastructure, attempt a semantic alteration where the content is attached at will, they are still invested in the modernist genealogy by their *tabula rasa* tendencies.

Para-city is imagined as a system of programmatically neutral habitats that situates itself dialectically to the tendencies of the Modernist projects and has the capacity to locate sites and proliferate in the varied and complex geometrical and cultural constructions of the present Metropolis.

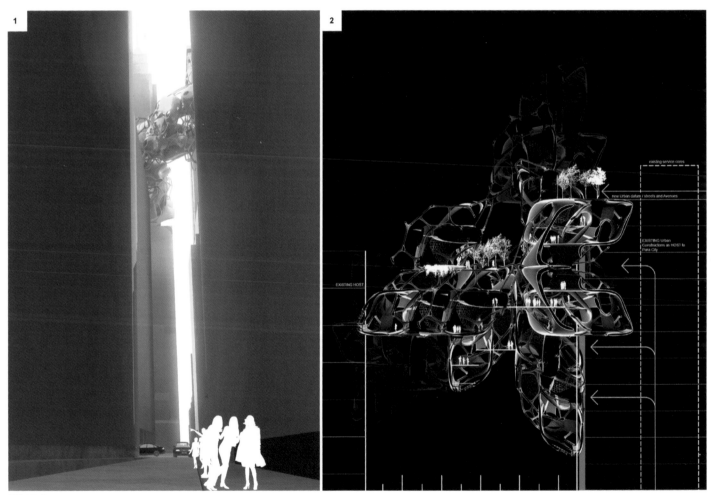

1 Street view
2 Conceptual section

With ever- increasing densities and changing programs, Para-city grows in the entire three-dimensional space of its host; the existing skyscrapers of the present urban landscape. Para-city feeds on the service-cores of its host, since sufficient service spaces already exist within the host-structure, to potentially free itself as a program-less ludic-zone, implying a radical overcoming of any spatial hierarchy; an architectural assemblage for a nomadic generation, where work and play coincide in nebulous zones of continuously shifting technological and cultural flows.

Para city is explicit as a version towards a progressive utopia that seeks 'play' between the totalizing form of the city and organicist individualism. The 'play' suggested here has its origins in the idea of the 'event'; " the moment of erosion, collapse, questioning, or problematization of the very assumptions of the setting within which a drama may take place-occasioning the chance or possibility of another, different setting." [as described by Foucault and further incorporated into the architectural discourse by Tschumi (Architecture and Disjunction)]. The future of architectural utopia is imagined in the facilitation of such play, implying a constant rupture and its immediate resolution… *ad infinitum*. An infinite feedback loop of perpetual anguish and its continual absorption.

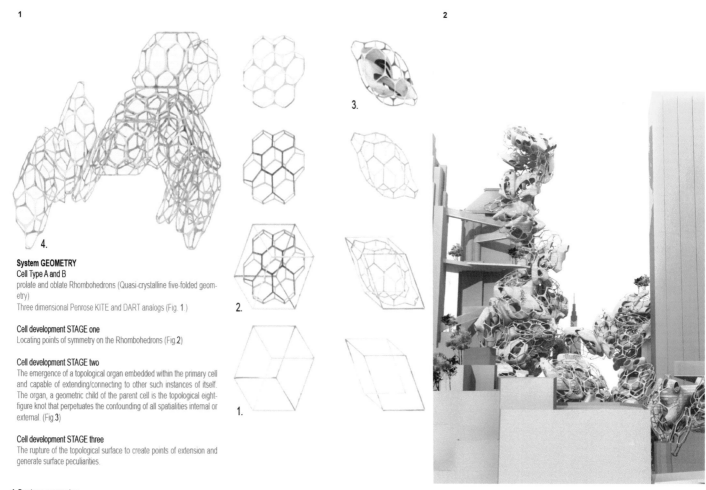

1

2

3.

4.

System GEOMETRY
Cell Type A and B
prolate and oblate Rhombohedrons (Quasi-crystalline five-folded geometry)
Three dimensional Penrose KITE and DART analogs (Fig. 1.)

Cell development STAGE one
Locating points of symmetry on the Rhombohedrons (Fig.2)

Cell development STAGE two
The emergence of a topological organ embedded within the primary cell and capable of extending/connecting to other such instances of itself. The organ, a geometric child of the parent cell is the topological eight-figure knot that perpetuates the confounding of all spatialities internal or external. (Fig.3)

Cell development STAGE three
The rupture of the topological surface to create points of extension and generate surface peculiarities.

1 System geometry
2 Perspective

>AN INVERTED SKYSCRAPER TYPOLOGY

Yi Cheng Pan
United Kingdom

The past decades have seen the creation of major cities from scratch, at break-neck speed, through the endless proliferation of Skyscrapers. Shanghai, Guangzhou, Dubai, Singapore are mere specimens of such a milieu that is set to perpetuate and grow.

The mass production of this ubiquitous and definitive building type, that investors, planners, and government addictively rely on to achieve both market efficiency and the "landmark" effect in any new urban development, clearly exposes the very paralysis and inability of the state to imagine a new city that is not populated by high-rises.   However, the insistence of such an ambition consequentially culminates in an inflexible urban plan that hinges on "uncertain" investments, while indefinitely postponing and denying the participation of mid/small-range, often local, businesses from activating the site with more economical building types.

The total abdication of control for the *laissez faire* agglomeration of skyscrapers is no longer the solution. Instead, control should be localized and intensified typologically to give the "city" different types of buildings.

1 City of cultivated difference
2 Typological change process

To subvert the control of the skyscrapers over the ground plane from its endless proliferation, the strategy is to invert the skyscrapers' massing through the cultivation of multiple urban plans within the skyscraper type, hence not only releasing the ground plane for the immediate activation of a variety of smaller building types, but also creating multiple "clustered" volumes for increased partnership of public and private establishments.

The project resists the formation of a generic empire, a city entirely submitted to the discretions of the corporations, by providing an urban typological framework – The Inverted Skyscraper Typology, is committed to the cultivation of difference, through the coexistence and participation of multiple types and stakeholders.

1 Multi-layered urban model

"Although it owes much to its heritage in the American skyscraper, the contemporary "Euroscraper" is in need of a new expression, one that provides distance from the modernist orthodoxy of the 20th Century and is a critical response to the ornate and delirious notions of the 21st Century tall building that now proliferate in cities such as Shanghai, Kuala Lumpur and Beijing. The European urban dilemma is that while rightfully holding onto the notion that cultural difference will continue to prevail throughout the European urban landscape, a new economic imperative must somehow become evident and explicit on the global stage." Hani Rashid

The Void: defining space with space
The concept of emptiness as aesthetics, the void as negative space, as positive formal element was borrowed from Isamu Noguchi's theoretical interests, a growth upward of earth-generated forces. He intended to capture the void, the immaterial by emptying the space of mass. The idea of framing the space or the city is also present in two examples in Paris: *Arc de Triomphe* and *La Defense*. Both entities seem to be interacting and framing one another. By designing a looped shape, a dialogue within the building itself, and between the building and nature, is achieved. The project basically filled space with space, rather than piercing it with a needle-like structure. The building was able to look at itself, understand itself, as a unified entity, as a belt, a city within a city; it is a single, unending surface. Weight and mass were replaced by light, time, and space.

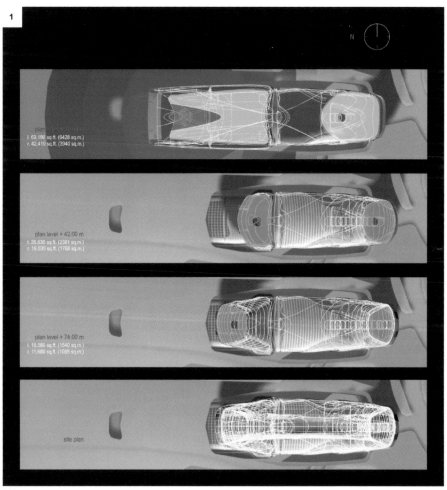

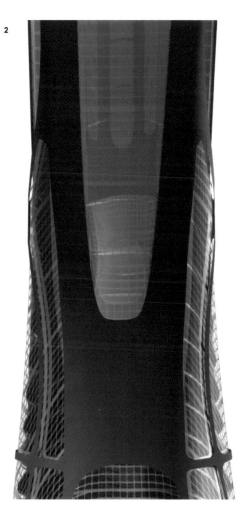

1 Plans
2 Structural skin

The formal scheme not only generated a coherent geometry to engage the flow of program and people, but also gave a new interpretation to the concepts of base, shaft, and crown, which are present in every single tall building.   Keeping the idea of the base as a more horizontal-oriented element, which actually interacts with the city while forming a natural departure for the shafts, it still anchors the building to the metropolitan fabric. The shaft, which basically ties the earth with the sky, appears bifurcated while redirecting upwards, a configuration that offers variety in floor plate shapes. When the shafts become one, the presence of the crown is addressed in an unusual way; the crown resembles horizontality in the endeavor of gaining more area at the top, which is meant for public spaces.

Structural Skin: questioning the central-cored, four-curtain-walled orthogonal scheme
Unlike traditional buildings , which use vertical supports, in this design the principal structural elements are central ring-like core and diagonally steel elements that spiral around the outer edge of the project. The aerodynamic form encourages wind to flow around its face, minimizing wind load on the structure and cladding. Natural air movement around the building generates substantial pressure difference across its face, which can be used to facilitate natural ventilation. This first building is not a traditional tower, but a continuous loop of horizontal and vertical sections that establish an urban site rather than a point in the sky.

1

1 Euroscraper in Port Malliot, Paris

>ZERO RESTRAIN MOBILITY
Alternatives to vertical circulation strategies within high-rises

Eduardo McIntosh
United Kingdom

The phenomenon of the "high-rise" can be read as a result of either high concentration of population or as a symbol of power and wealth. In any case, if we put structural issues out of the equation it is clear that the key element that enabled the birth of the skyscraper was the invention of the elevator. Therefore, it is ironic that the elevator is precisely what has totally limited the evolution of high-rise buildings in terms of programmatic and formal alternatives.

Many attempts have been made to try to escape the ubiquitous tower typology. Yona Friedman's utopian inhabitable porticoes and interconnected towers, Moshe Safdie's scattered prisms, and Arata Isozaki's branching tree-like buildings, are a few of the most radical and original alternatives. Nevertheless, despite their seemingly dissimilar nature, they have one common omnipresent condition, the concentration of the vertical circulation, be it in the form of staircases or mechanical devices. The elevator, because of its capability of movement, is mistakenly perceived as a liberating agent. On closer inspection, its range of movement is totally limited by its encasing. It is particularly interesting to see that this encasing not only holds down the elevator form mutating, but by doing so, also constrains the possibilities of evolution of the building. One other interesting example is the case of Plug-in City by Archigram, where the mechanical device that governs the mega structure is a crane set on a railway.

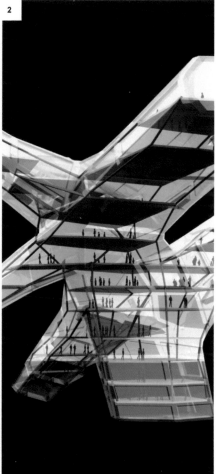

1 Environment interaction
2 Module

The hovercraft is a transportation device that can negotiate almost any terrain and that is totally independent of the structure. Is this exogenous element a form of "architecture"? That question is irrelevant. The important issue is that a mechanical device for moving people within a building could liberate this building from the constraints imposed by the vertical circulation shaft. My proposition is to separate the vertical circulation from the main structure of the building. To do so, I plan to take the idea of the crane and liberate it form the railway by grouping several cranes into an autonomous free moving device that could roam along the exterior of the building by clinging to appendices scattered on its surface while carrying users or items inside capsules. The agents would work as a system that would be governed by a minimal route algorithm (e.g. ant colony optimization algorithm) to improve every users travel time. Power would be provided to these agents through the appendices on the buildings surface. This type of displacement also has the advantage of providing quick evacuation capabilities from every part of the building.

Due to the fact that there would no longer be a need for the building to conform to the shape and use dictated by the vertical shaft, the high-rise could grow in a more organic fashion, adopting the shape of any given space, and growing as needed by consumer demand. The building is no longer a dead, static shell, but a living entity that negotiates between our needs and the surrounding environment.

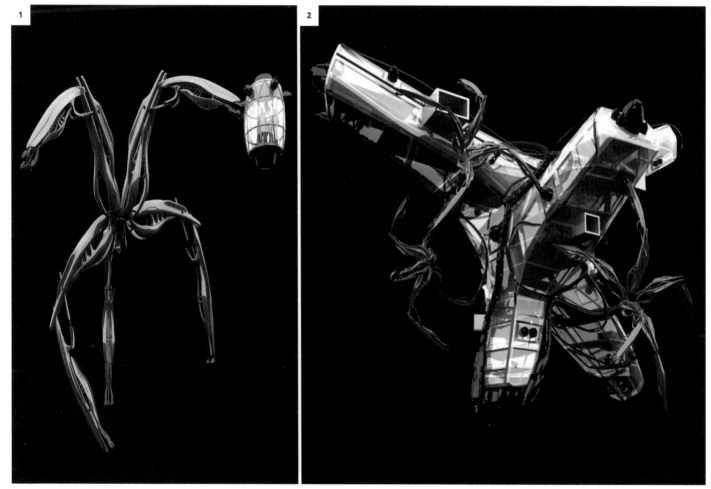

1 Detached circulation
2 Module infrastructure

Sentina is an abandoned and degraded place situated in Italy's west coast. The space dimension of this almost uncontaminated landscape needs a new construction that takes into consideration history and nature.

Our project traces a track of this landscape, a linear axis, a mixture of history and contemporary life: a route that highlights the presence of ancient country houses and an axis that ends unavoidably at the sea. Therefore the road as a bi-dimensional entity is transformed into a three-dimensional element, thanks to a vertically constructed space. Detaching itself from earth, it partly contains a route equipped with mastings, a canal, sporting and playing areas.

As it meets the line of the sea, the road bends, transforming into a skyscraper, which is one hundred and fifty meters high. It is an element which, without any mediation between the space and the surrounding nature, establishes a pure and decisive contrast between horizontal and vertical, between nature and artifice, between ancient and modern. The skyscraper contains lodging, services, communal and exhibition spaces, shops, and restaurants.

1 Apartments
2 Cross section

1 Aerial view
2 Recreational areas

>SKYSCRAPER IN PARIS

Xavier Lagurgue, Günther Domenig
France

While the first skyscraper projects emerge on the circular Parisian highway, with the aim to densify the agglomeration and preserve the historical center, we propose to set up a network of towers which we call biotopes. The smallest ones are higher than the Eiffel Tower. It's a "building provocation", or as the artist Tatiana Trouvé would say, "a paradoxical injunction in which different types of urban organization, although incompatible at the first sight, are superposed".

When towers are built above the old city, the town as a whole changes and becomes a new one as the result of the dialogue between the contemporary vertical towers and the old horizontal city. The old town does not exist any more in the same way, although it is still there. The background of this paradox is to question our position as users of urban space. It allows us to place ourselves in a sustainable urban development perspective and set priorities: construction, society, economy, environment, history, aesthetics.

We propose to change the status of historical city centers by renewing their accommodation capacity and their evolution potential, rather than accelerate the « museification » of them. This always generates the decline of the suburbs, which are considered to be ideal for experimenting new urban forms. By doing so, the old town is serving as an enormous network of roots for the above located mega-systems, which are covering it and radically transforming its perception. It is only from that starting point that one can imagine building similar constructions in the suburbs.

1

2

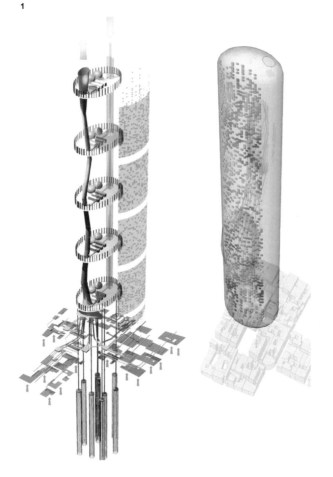

1 Concept diagram
2 Paris 2240

Rather than being in favor of the uncontrolled expansion of cities - one of the major reasons for the increase in pollution and energy consumption - we propose to make the old city center denser, by superposing several layers which will multiply the actual capacity by ten. We postulate that the old town with its historical diversity, but also with its transportation networks, its energy consumption, and its exclusive relationship with all forms of life, is an obsolete model for the future evolution and is contributing to today's environmental situation.

Finally, instead of raising the center of Paris as *Le Corbusier* intended in 1925 with his "*Plan voisin*", we propose to superpose the existing with new layers of buildings, which are conceived for a long term life cycle, taking into consideration the future urban development of several centuries, but keeping the preservation of history as a fundamental principle.

We are all sensitive to what the architects Decostered and Rham call the "temptation of the heritage" but, with the perspective of global warming we believe that the idea of "freezing" the cultural heritage of old cities in order to continue expansion is not justified and is based on a short term vision. Therefore, on a theoretical level, the physical limits of the "vertical biotope" are articulated around three complementary principles which are known since 1950 and proposed by Buckminster Fuller in his giant dome covering the city: the capacity to increase the building surface, the autonomous energy system, the independency concerning the climactic and biological aspects.

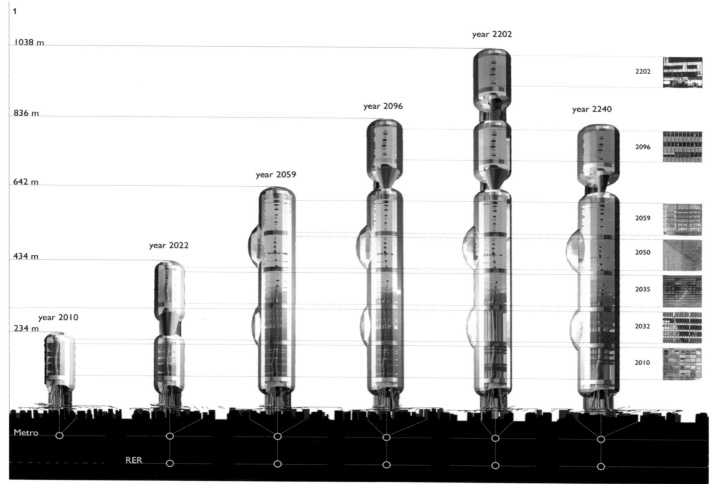

1 Skyscraper time-line

>SKYSCRAPER IN HONG KONG

Su Hou Chen, Melinda Sanes,
Neil Cook
United States

Undeveloped land is scarcely available in Hong Kong, the densest urban area in the world. In the Western, Central and Wan Chai districts, this has historically led to the in-fill of Victoria Harbor and the creation of an artificial shoreline. This continued way of development replaces harbor with hardscape, further compounding the negative ecological consequences of unintelligent waterfront development, namely, added water pollution, increased impervious surface area, and reduced light exposure to the channel bottom.

A series of preliminary structural explorations led to the development of initial programmatic opportunities and constraints; the basic structural part of an oscillating system was formulated based on iterative massing models. Structural components were accumulated to fill out the general massing of tower height and width, and then modified locally to increase stability. Elements of the structural system were then thickened, multiplied, eroded, or atrophied based on a series of physical modeling experiments designed to expose structural redundancies and weaknesses. As such, a materially efficient structural design emerged. Areas of greatest promise and latent multivalence were selected and explored as detail areas. The entire tower was then revised and reaccumulated based on micro-scale structural and enclosure principles, site and contextual concerns, and overall vertical and lateral gradients of density, porosity, and opacity. These many sets of systems play themselves out through the tower, vertically mixing with each other, creating a truly novel spatiality, not present in traditional adaptations of the vertical building.

1

2

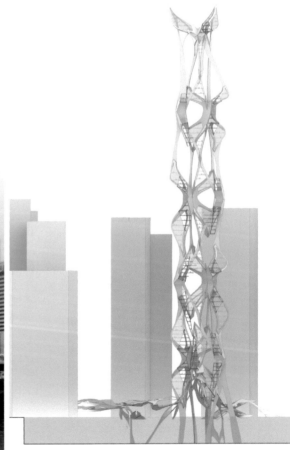

1 View from Victoria Harbor
2 Cross section

The tower's primary structural system is conceived of as a lattice of alternating space-frame elements (pods) and planar elements (fins). The primary vertical structure oscillates between the interior and exterior of the tower, changing at moments of movement between spatial zones; the primary lateral structure has two components: the structural sleeve of interconnected pods, dealt primarily with rotational stability, and the crisscrossed lateral 'braid', dealt mainly with swaying and overturning. The systems are attenuated to their contextual situation, on the northeastern, harbor-facing side of the tower, the surfaces of the lattice multiply and expand vertically to create larger areas of contiguous facade, sheltering the interior open space from the strong prevailing winds. On the southwestern, urban side, the lattice surfaces pull back from each other, exposing the interior gallery and park system, and opening views between the interior of the tower and the city.

The circulatory system is composed of axial banks of elevators meeting periodically at universal floors, which connect to all banks laterally around the tower. At these floors, one may proceed into the localized circulatory systems or switch elevators to continue vertically up the tower. The local systems are composed of gallery stairs, egress stairs and localized elevators - a loop of exterior stairs, galleries, and interior pavilions, winds its way vertically through the tower, attaching itself to the primary vertical fins and the lateral braid. These gallery stairs become the vertical pathway system of the park, allowing access to the park from selected floors, and closing down at times for security.

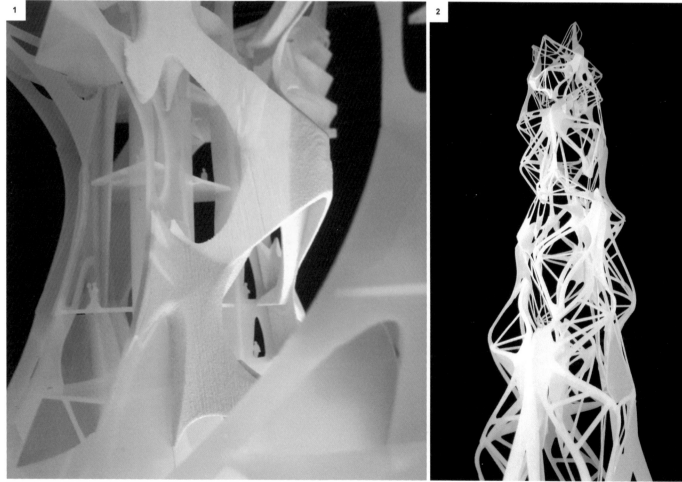

1 Model detail
2 Structure model

>GENO-MATRIX

Ming Tang, Dihua Yang
United States

The traditional skyscraper is no longer a valid response to the dynamic demands of the XXI Century, due to its limited and static form which is incapable of adapting to changing contextual parameters. The central feature of our project is the development of a deformable structure that exhibits characteristics of a living organism, with the potential for evolution, in a manner similar to the larger cityscape. We named it: "Geno-Matrix", a genotype driven structure for skyscraper which, according to the changing spatial requirements, can produce potentially infinite scenarios. It can deform itself in the molecular level, compatible with the unstable fitness of current inhabitation cultures. Rather than using the conversional architectural design process to generate the form, Geno-Matrix comes from genotype, phenotype, mate, crossover, morph, mutation, and selection process. Geno-Matrix can be adapted to any context and multiplied throughout the urban space. In the design process, we applied genetic computing and evolution techniques with the emphasis on their potential of creating forms that are useful in the production of architectural innovation.

Inspired by the Lego blocks, the strategy of Geno-Matrix is to do as much pre-fabrication as possible, under controlled factory conditions. Within a modular building system, large quantity of cubic units are fabricated and assembled into a lattice system. These units can be "pulled", "pushed" or "combined" in the lattice grid along the axis and form infinite typological features. The characteristic of the skyscraper heavily relies on these units' location and the internal logic between them. The skyscraper is formed by the same building "blocks" that takes on an organization imposed by the social, economic, and culture requirements of the site.

1

Modular system
Inspired by the Lego blocks, the strategy of Geno-Matrix is to do as much pre-fabrication as possible, under controlled factory conditions. Within a modular building system, large quantity of cubic units are fabricated and assembled into a lattice system. These units can be "pulled", "pushed" or "combined" in the lattice grid along the axis and form infinite typological features

Molecular zoning
While molecularisation allows for units assembly from the bottom-up, the linear hierarchy are replaced by more complex network. In our project, we are investigating the relationships between the units. By Occupation, habitation, lifestyle, need, and economy are reflected in this skin. For instance, grid like pattern repeats the grid of the streets, and small-scale living units can be combined to form large-scale commercial units. Overlapping multiple patterns forms the potential mixed-use zones, which can be continuously configures based on the changing spatial requirement over years.

1 Concept diagram

While molecularization allows for units' assembly from the bottom-up, the linear hierarchy is replaced by more complex network. In our project, we are investigating the relationships between the units. Occupation, habitation, lifestyle, need, and economy are reflected in this skin. For instance, grid like pattern repeats the grid of the streets, and small-scale living units can be combined to form large-scale commercial units. Overlapping multiple patterns form the potential mixed-use zones, which can be continuously configured based on the changing spatial requirements over the years.

By changing local relationships of individual units, Geno-Matrix can affect an emotional response, similar to that realized by the culture icon or national symbol, though on a much larger scale. For instance, to reflect the social value, an ordinary "tree" pattern can be generated by moving the units along the normal axis. Organization patterns emerge at varying scale and hierarchy.

Since Charles Darwin proposed his theory stating that all species are generated via the process of evolution, and genetic approach is now considered not only powerful enough to solve biological puzzles, but also useful in the simulation of creating algorithms and 3D graphics for higher level of complexity and diversity. Within the evolution hierarchy all individual features are condensed and passed to the next generation. Here, variations can simply take place by changing the crossover rule in hierarchy, or introducing a new genotype into the system. With GE, designers could yield novel, creative design solutions based on the mixture of several existing successful cases.

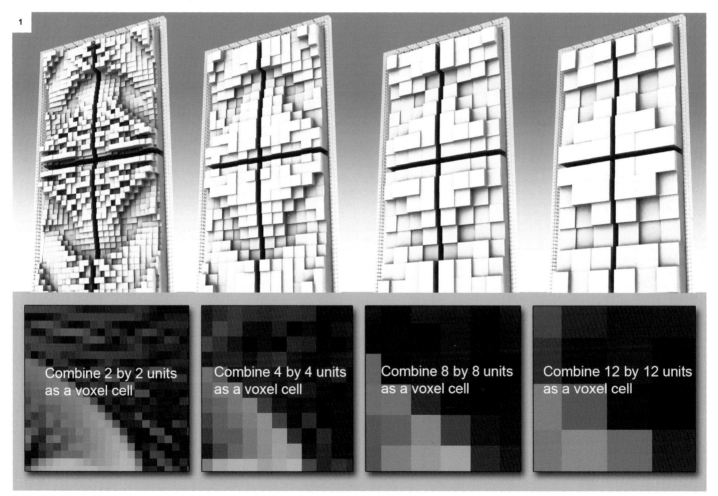

1

Combine 2 by 2 units as a voxel cell

Combine 4 by 4 units as a voxel cell

Combine 8 by 8 units as a voxel cell

Combine 12 by 12 units as a voxel cell

1 Potential units configuration

>COMPRESSED COMPLEXITY
Multi Functional High Rise Structure

Eldine Heep, Gerhild Orthacker
Judith Schafelner, Elle Przybyla
Austria

Contemporary urban scenarios

The contemporary urban landscape, with its overlay of extensive freeway systems and infrastructures for mobility, can be viewed as an expanse of built form and its spatial residuum. These territories of voids are not planned in so much as they are generated by the changing morphology of the urban grid. Rather than resist or 'correct' these entropic tendencies that occur in the horizontal plane, the project seeks to embody them in a vertical, architectural scenario. As an urban model, the multi-functional high rise, with its mix of commercial, office, and residential programs, has the potential to dynamically engage in the spatial complexities that characterize the contemporary urban grid. By moving away from the notion of the fixed skyscraper, a functionally stratified structure that compartmentalizes program into predictable discrete zones, the proposal presents a systematic methodology for programmatic hybridization.

Typologies

Each program was assessed to determine how it operated in the horizontal field, with particular attention to accessibility, proximal relationships, and visibility. Residential, office, and shopping grid configurations can be said to have either a closed or open quality. Borrowing from network theory[2], in which systems can be defined as centralized (more closed, based on a single node) or distributed (more open, based on multiple nodes), the programs were assigned network values to describe access.

1

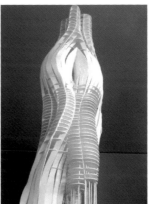

2

1 Physical model
2 Facade detail

The development of new program typologies, based on centralized or distributed access, establishes a unifying principle that applies to all programs equally. With their radial organization and focus on pathways, the diagrammatic plans for the different typologies can be recombined and, therefore, allow for the evolutionary development of vertical interconnectivity.

Structure and form

The primary structure, a bundling tubular system, consists of three tubes, each with a central core that runs from ground to top. Where the circulation distributes into multiple cores (resulting from the introduction of a distributed typology), two tubes merge and two programs are connected. In these areas of programmatic overlap, voids with different levels of interconnectivity emerge; this interconnectivity depends on the program mix. Where two tubes merge, the third remains independent with one central core (thus, maintaining its centralized typology). In the tower, each tube connects with the other two at one or more points. Because the tubes buttress each other, the floor plates can remain relatively small, despite the building's height. The secondary structure, a transformative system, is articulated differently throughout the building, according to programmatic demands.

1 Pope, Albert. Ladders. Houston, Tex.: Rice School of Architecture; New York: Princeton Architectural Press, 1996.

2 Barabasi, Albert-Lazlo. Linked: The New Science of Networks. Cambridge, Mass.: Perseus Publishing, 2002.

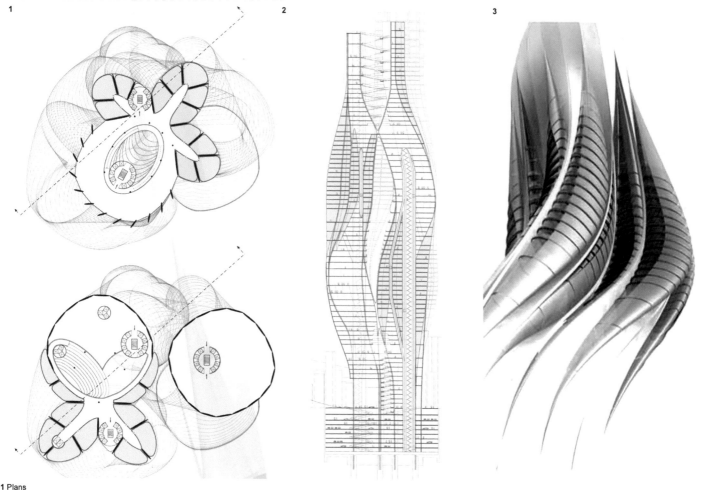

1

2

3

1 Plans
2 Cross section
3 Facade detail

Dominiki Dadatsi, Fountoulaki Elrini
Pavlidou Eleni
Greece

This tower is a case study of a larger housing proposal situated in East London that serves as an example of adaptive architecture. Based on ecological systems, the team investigates how an urban development can be explored as a simulation model of natural growth that negotiates and adapts to the existing urban fabric. Borrowing rules and functions from the natural world, such as growth and phyllotaxis, the project is an investigation of parametric development adapting to different urban needs.

The project aims to create an open parametric system, towers as vertical urbanism, capable of adjusting to different conditions. It explores how to produce architectural forms based on understanding and simulating the people's behavior and movement inside the urban fabric. For that reason, the team uses an agent based system as a generative method of design. Based on five different categories of users: students, business people, travellers, artists and academics; five different behaviors of movement are simulated, based on the characteristics of each type. The system is also informed by the data of the surrounding area (attractions, obstacles, access points, and infrastructure) creating the general urban field and vertical paths for the generation of the towers. Internally, two types of circulation are proposed; the first one is a vertical circulation that follows the paths of the tower and distributes the users into the units, and the second one is a helical model of circulation that defines the public realm of the building.

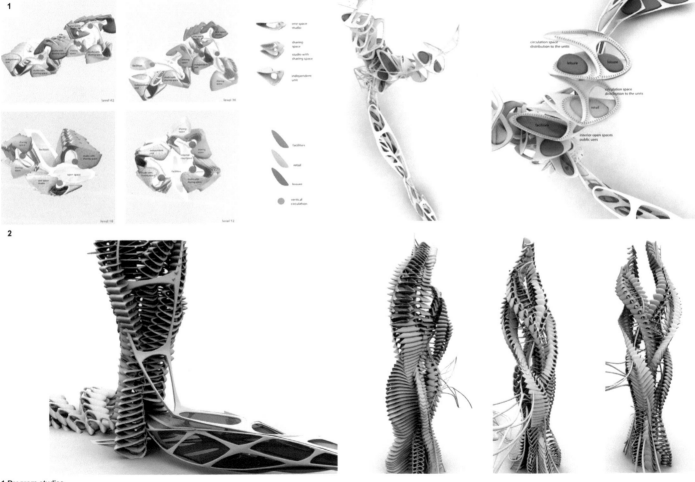

1 Program studies
2 Perspectives

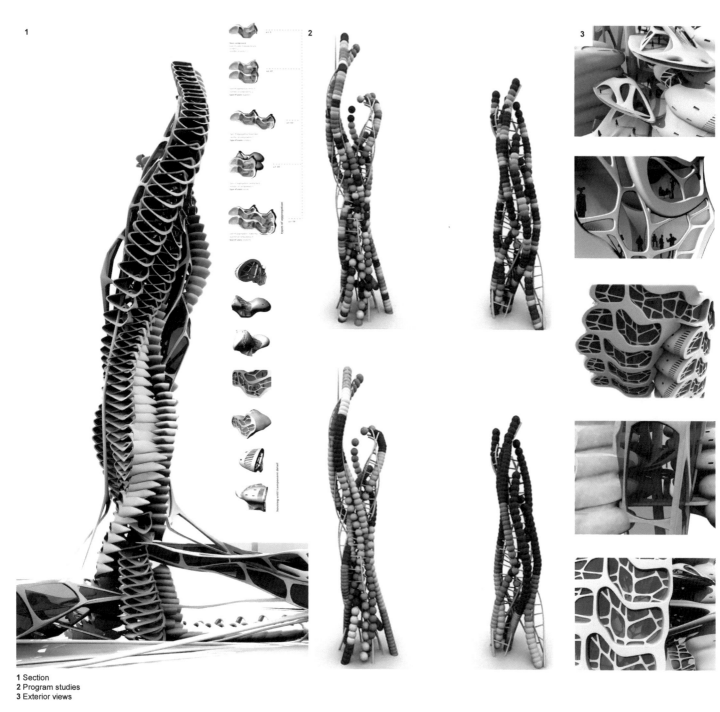

1 Section
2 Program studies
3 Exterior views

>QUANTUM CITY

Sebastien Chauvel
France

Thinking about the city in two dimensions means a horizontal spreading of the urban mass, an estrangement of the functions and a loss of social cohesion. The urban scattering creates a waste of energy, space, and resources. The compact urban planning in three dimensions, such as the skyscraper, offers a solution to these problems.

The theoretical ideal city is not one in three dimensions but rather the quantum city. The quantum state shows itself in the sub-atomic scale as the property of a particle to exist in an infinite number of states, everywhere and nowhere at the same time. The quantum city would be characterized by the plurality of its different and superimposed realities. It is the city of the possible integration of the principles of compactness and durability.

The project is located on Saya de Malha's sandbank. For foundation it has a structural grid of nanotubes in geostationary balance. It allows structural and stiffening elements by a semiautomatic assembly platform. The secondary structure is an endo-skeleton that will allow the organization of islands and public areas. The main materials for construction are taken from the site, essentially sand and calcareous substratum.

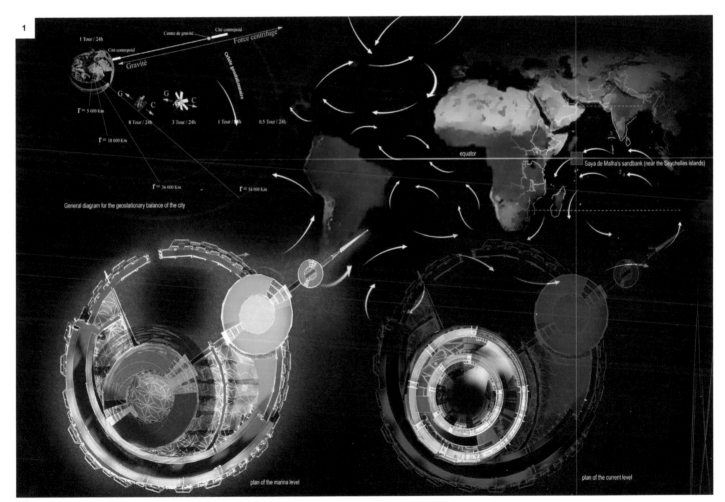

1 Project location, plans

The city is organized as an organism divided in sectors. The first one is the skeleton which houses the energy production and transportation systems. The second one is a skin that covers the entire city with housing, offices, shops and recreational areas. Every sector is an appendix, autonomous but in constant flux with the rest of the city.

The project swirls around a central space of 120 meters in diameter. A thermal chimney with wind turbines will provide energy to the entire city. Magnetic elevators will serve the city horizontally and vertically. Approximately 72 elevators for 250 people, will connect the entire city; secondary elevators will be located along the external skin.

The public space is a continuous band from the bottom to the top of the building, where life takes place, with access to offices, retail, and amenities. It is also the expression of the community, encouraging the urban culture and the creation of citizenship.

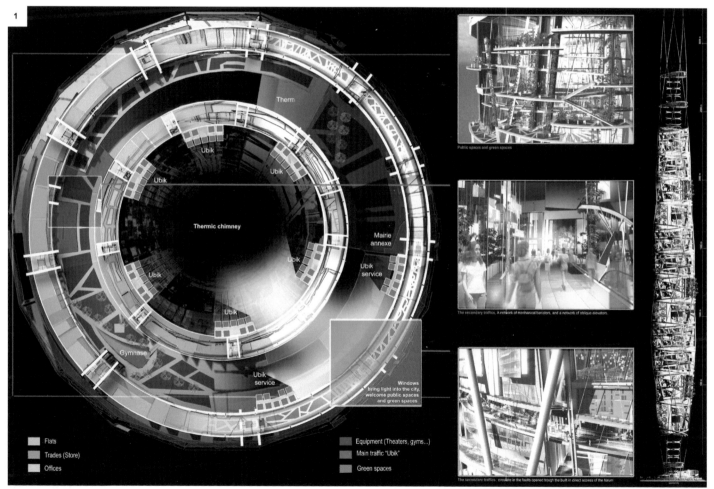

1 Program plan, section

The Ritual Towers are multi-purpose structures, challenging wood architecture to produce an iconic and green project. Designed to aid small towns in poverty, the towers are located in the Pentecost Islands.

The design generates power and pumps fresh usable water, at the same time it can be used for the Naghol leaping rituals. The iconic shape comes from the idea of energy in the form of a flame. The design is composed by two towers. The first tower is the wind tower, with turbines that generate energy. The second tower is the water tower and reservoir.

To better understand the context, the island is pure virgin land. Therefore, placing a self powered water tower is fit for this natural habitat. The tower is made exclusively of wood and is tied together with steel connections, rope, and vine, for structural support; with the beauty of vernacular architecture.

The skin is made of twisted vine found on the island, which is the same vine used to jump off of the tower. The vine skin will also eventually grow foliage, which will climb and cover the whole tower. In the end, a design for the land diving Naghol ritual.

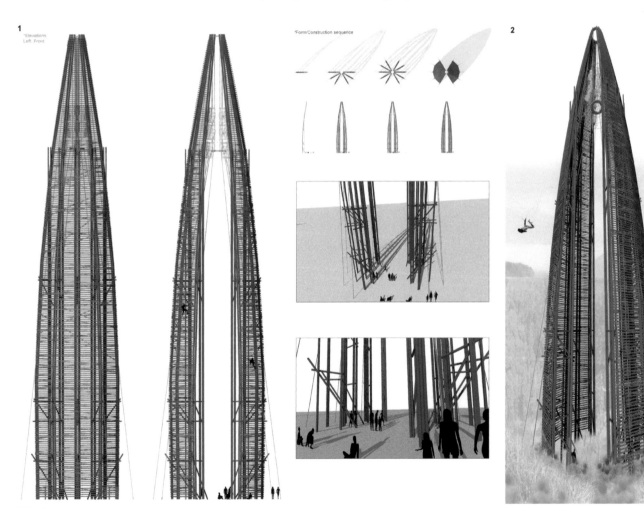

1 Elevations, construction process
2 Perspective

1 Seasonal plant growth
2 Platform views

Paula Tomisaki
United States

>CHIMERA
Hybrid city

The complexities and the dynamism of contemporary life cannot be cast into the simple platonic forms provided by the classical canon, nor does the modern style afford enough means of articulation. We have to deal with social diagrams that are more complex when compared with the social programs of the early modern period. Instead of forcing the program to fill spaces of a static typology, a revision and expansion of the skyscraper is considered. The project "Chimera" challenges typological classification. Chimera is a name borrowed from the hybrid mythological creature made of parts of multiple animals. The hybrid acknowledges and celebrates the heterogeneity and complexity of our world.

The project emerges from an instrumental hybridization process, leading to programmatic invention and the emergence of novel and unpredictable possibilities through new instances of adjacency, overlapping and cross-breeding. It is an attempt to replace deterministic notions of causality (prescribed architecture) with a bottom-up, non-linear design process. This proposal is set up to explore the behavior of programs combination and large scale architectonic issues. The project is a 60,000 sqm cultural and commercial Free Trade Zone in Athens, Greece.

Chimera is based on the idea of intertwined programmatic elements in a consistent whole. It is a dynamic hybrid that through specific fusions and mutations of commercial and cultural functions and unprecedented new spaces, create a synergy, a new organization whose unity produces a whole greater than the sum of its parts.

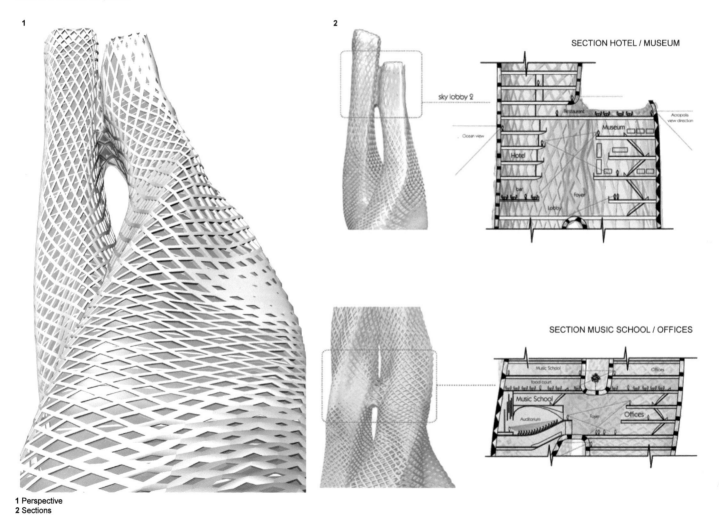

1 Perspective
2 Sections

Genetic Skin. Providing completely free plans to accommodate in a flexible manner, the variety of programs, including structure, enclosure, facilities and circulations, became a composite skin. The exoskeleton is generated by an algorithm which grows the skin cells in width and thickening, responding to its content and context. The skin became the input for greater specialization and local differentiation through the transmission of its attributes. Stress intensity acts as feedback for the exoskeleton's design. The morphological continuity provides structural integrity, and a parametric model allows for the accurate actualization of the exoskeleton geometry. This structural net has two main reactive behaviors derived from the typological hybridization. On the one hand, in the vertical section the load vectors are distributed by splitting the effort thru the diagrid diagram, avoiding "breaking moments" in the skin. On the other hand, the horizontal section of the structural net acts according to the principle of "compression arcs", which allows hanging the concert hall from the structure, generating a surrounding buffer zone.

Topology vs Typology. The topological approach produces a shift of emphasis from form to the structure(s) of relations, interconnections that exist internally and externally within an architectural project. This project addresses the organic as a mechanism that allows multiplicity and not typological classifications.

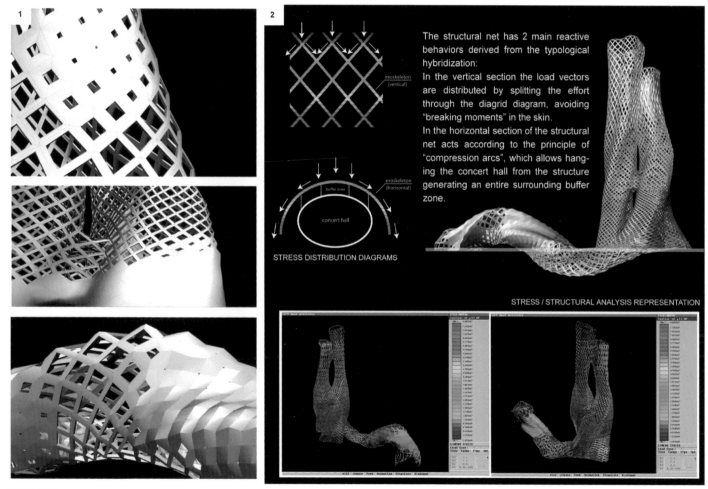

The structural net has 2 main reactive behaviors derived from the typological hybridization:

In the vertical section the load vectors are distributed by splitting the effort through the diagrid diagram, avoiding "breaking moments" in the skin.

In the horizontal section of the structural net acts according to the principle of "compression arcs", which allows hanging the concert hall from the structure generating an entire surrounding buffer zone.

STRESS DISTRIBUTION DIAGRAMS

STRESS / STRUCTURAL ANALYSIS REPRESENTATION

1 Structural skin
2 Structural skin analysis

>WARP
A vertical deformation of time / space

Nenand Basic, Keeyong Lee
Bosnia Hercegovina / South Korea

The project questions the possibility of coexistence between a high-rise building and a horizontal city. It is placed in a typical Western European city, characterized by high density of historic urban fabric, materialized in the historic Place des Vosges, in Paris, France. Any kind of intervention here seems impossible...

Finding a way to integrate the high-rise building into this urban tissue, and at the same time provide it with minimum impact to the surroundings, while giving it maximum surface / program capability, is the main objective. We wanted to avoid the usual way of imagining skyscrapers, the one that imposes its own, strange, and often totalitarian law.

The solution comes from an old anatomy book showing sections of the human body, where a thin foot holds a huge body above ground. The building is composed of three independent steel structures rising from different places within the chosen neighborhood. They come together in a unique building once the desired height has been reached. Climbing over the existing surrounding buildings, this structure serves as a base for the implementation of various programs, disposed in a hectic way, exactly like the more usual, horizontal city.

1

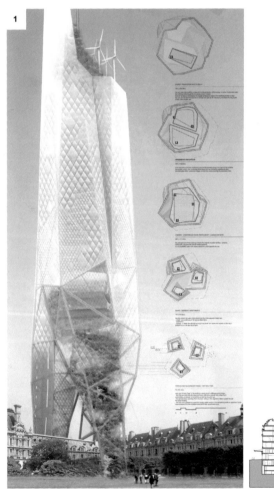

2

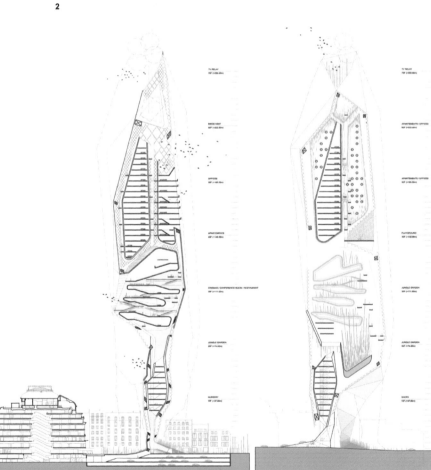

1 Perspective, plans
2 Sections

The lower parts of the three structures create programmatic and typological links within the existing neighborhood. A series of shops and small public amenities serve as connecting vectors, leading the users into the heights of the building. On the ground every independent structure fuses with its surroundings. On one side, the city climbs on it; benches, pavement, street lights colonize it, following the vertical deformation of the city. On the other, nature takes its share of the newly conquered city space. The neighboring park invades one of the individual structures and leads nature to the very core of the building. A series of cores are developed within the structure each having different functions and typologies of spaces. These cores form independent units within the global building. Each has its own facade, its own rules. The whole is wrapped in a global external skin, which is neither air nor water proof. It is made out of ETFE (ethylene-tetraflouroethylene) panels. They play a double role, unifying this heteroclit environment and producing energy. The large surfaces of ETFE facade protect the inside from the strong winds and at the same time let the air and the rain pass through.

Under the facade large surfaces are covered with solar cells. The presence of ETFE improves their capacity of energy production by 20%. The top part of the building contains a field of wind mills, supplying the needed energy for the building.

1

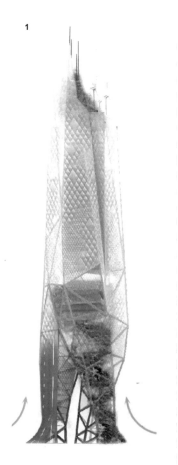
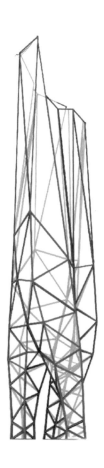

GLOBAL CONCEPT   STRUCTURE   PROGRAM   SKIN

1 Concept diagrams

Along with space tourism and adventurous tourist destinations, the Waterscraper offers an opportunity to experience the world's most voluminous element – water and its amazing habitat. Built as a skyscraper upside-down, into the sea, the Waterscraper creates a habitable link towards the lower levels of the sea and features a unique hotel with a distinctive combination of recreation and scientific facilities.

Half building and half vessel, the Waterscraper's design and construction is purely driven by the analysis of aquatic forces. The circular setting provides an effective ring structure to withstand the water pressure. The floor plates diminish in size as the water pressure rises in the lower levels. The submerged main body is stabilized by the floating ring which connects via a dampened bridge structures to ensure the vertical position of the Waterscaper at all times.

The architecture follows the structural requirements and emphasizes this by allocating a distinctive use to the different design elements of the Waterscraper. The main cone reaches down 400 ft. and provides a mix of hotel rooms, laboratories, green rooms and a viewing platform at 25 floors below the sea level.

1 Above water view

A glazed dome marks the top of the structure and allows light to penetrate deep into the inner atrium, which connects the public and private zones of the hotel facilities. While the hotel's lobby, restaurant and café are situated in the levels above the sea, the conference facilities and hotel rooms are located below sea level with a view into the vivid underwater world.

The surrounding ring accommodates a series of apartments with direct access to the Waterscraper's beaches. Eight beach platforms are hung between the bridging elements of the structure and are directed towards the centre to form a protected water area within the open sea. Further the ring encloses the Waterscraper's marina and connects to the main plaza in front of the dome. The space below the plaza is used for the compounds own underwater port and diving center.

The Waterscraper is a floating building. It can drift within the open sea, move to a different location or it can anchor to achieve a fixed position. Currently a handful of motivated engineers have started to investigate the buoyancy relations and structural response to the enormous water pressure. If this proves feasible the Waterscraper may well become reality one day.

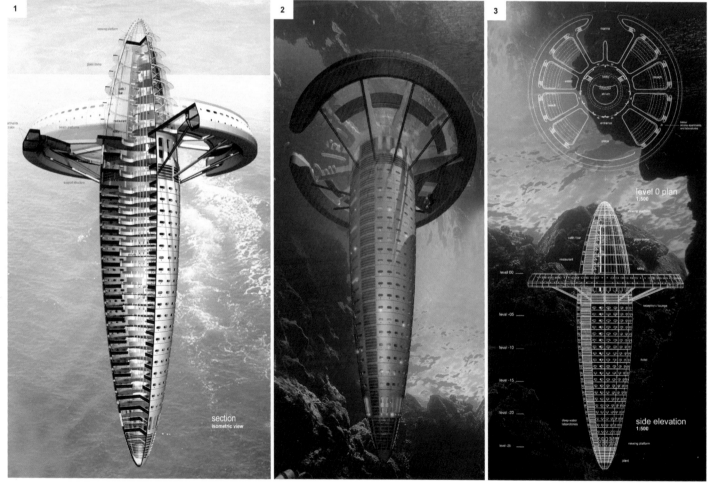

1 Program section
2 Underwater view
3 Plan, section

>PHARE TOWER

Manuelle Gautrand
France

Client : Unibail,
Name / Location : « Tour Phare », La Défense district in Paris - France
Dates : international competition: 2006
Area : 140.000 m², High : 300 m
Construction Cost: 500 M€
Consultants: Jacobs France, Terrell International, Arcora, Alto Ingenierie,
Casso, Edeca, Tohier
Project Manager: Yves Tougard and Bertrand Colson
Images: Platform, Model Maker: New Tone

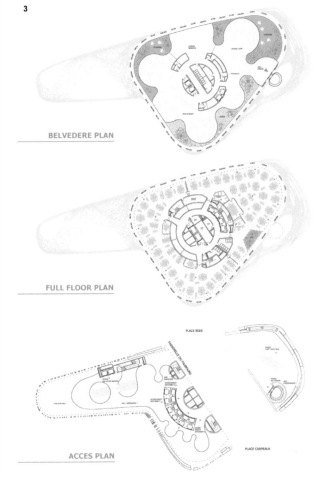

BELVEDERE PLAN

FULL FLOOR PLAN

ACCES PLAN

1 Street view
2 Model detail
3 Plans

Phare Tower is a 300 meter-high new-generation tower at *La Défense*, on the western rim of Paris, France. The program consists of 140 000 m^2 of office space with two restaurants and a rooftop viewing deck for the general public. The concept we are evolving aims at two things. First, express power in a high-rise structure that is a communication device without precedent. Second, introduce poetry by creating a unique building the size of the Eiffel Tower.

Structurally, the tower is designed as an externally exposed skeleton that wraps the office floors in a double-layer mesh of woven metal, lacquered two-tone, white and beige. Both meshes interlace via large circular openings that draw them together. This structural-skin soars up a thousand feet in graceful formal liberty, set free from the usual constraints that plague towers. In fact, it resolves itself on different scales: the individual scale of the offices, which makes them human while opening superb views over the cityscape; and the overall scale of structural might and outsized dimensions. At the foot of the tower, the interwoven mesh flares out to form large round openings that give ground-level space spectacular monumental presence on the esplanade.

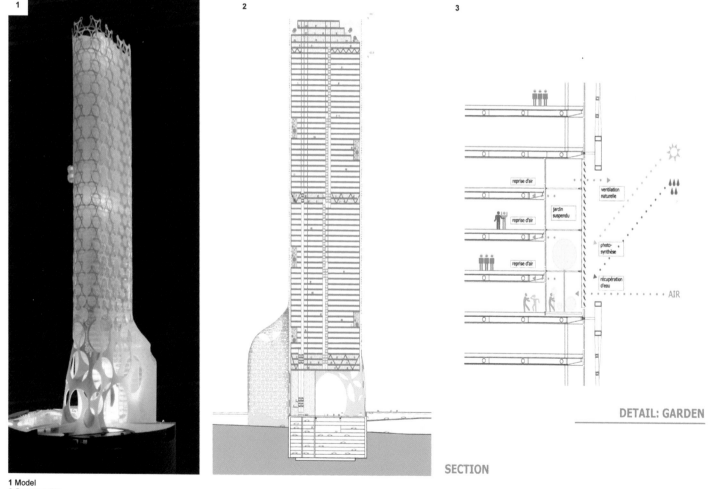

1 Model
2 Cross section
3 Facade detail

Drew Mills, Sebastian Messer,
Paul Warrior
United States

The problem

Central London is amongst the most expensive locations for land and real estate in the world despite having a 19th Century transportation system at full capacity that puts the city in danger of stagnating and losing its pre-eminent world city status. The long-delayed Cross Rail Project, which will form a rail link between Heathrow, Brentwood, and Shenfield, via the West End and Canary Wharf, will likely begin construction in 2008. It will not be completed until 2015, three years after the London Olympics.

It is hoped by its supporters, including the current UK Government, that Cross Rail will facilitate the development of Thames Gateway to address the chronic shortage of affordable housing in London. However, the environmental impact of a building program, on the 40 miles stretch from the Thames Barrier at Woolwich to the marshlands of the Thames Estuary in Kent, remains highly contentious. It also repeats a solution of the past by creating an underground network designed to distribute the population to the suburbs.

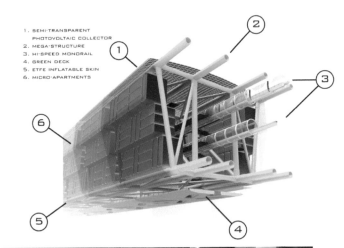

1. SEMI-TRANSPARENT PHOTOVOLTAIC COLLECTOR
2. MEGA-STRUCTURE
3. HI-SPEED MONORAIL
4. GREEN DECK
5. ETFE INFLATABLE SKIN
6. MICRO-APARTMENTS

1 Overground London
2 View from Thames River
3 Interior corridor

The solution

The solution to London's congestion is not underground, but London Overground. More easily and rapidly constructed than the tunnel which Cross Rail proposes from Paddington to the Isle of Dogs, a network of elevated, high speed rail connections, London Overground would be the armature for the construction of a mega-structure overlaying the historic city center.

London Overground would be financed by realizing air-rights developments off the structure and would contribute significantly to the solution of London's housing shortage through "planning gain" on commercial developments and the densification of the city center rather than the construction of a new suburb.

1 Station

>SKYSCRAPER ROOTS

Laurent Saint-Val
France

At a time when Mankind understands the need to respect and protect nature, in order to enable the continuation of life, architecture draws its inspiration from nature and attempts to use nature's energy in the most ecologically friendly manner.

A skyscraper cannot be built on a site as a vulgar object, without link with its urban environment; it must grow from the ground. Is there a tree without roots? To live, plants need to be in contact with the ground, so their roots draw water and rock salt necessary for their development. In the same manner, it seems to me that the new skyscraper needs to weave a link between the basement (its foundations), the ground, and the sky. The "roots" of the skyscraper come to collect the activity on the ground and carry it out in height. Its architecture is made up of several structural roots, of several branches which come to be rolled up between them. They absorb the urban landscape, and conversely the urban space creates them.

1 View from plaza
2 Elevation

The skyscraper of tomorrow comes to nourish activities of its urban environment and the ability to generate new activities. Thus, the basement shelters serve as shopping centers, or the access to the subway stations, and form a network of cavities which recall galleries of anthills. On the ground floor, the rhythm is slower; one finds areas for relaxation, open to the public as hanging gardens which climb on the members of the new building. As we continue our ascent, we gradually move to more private spaces: the flats.

The architecture of the building allows that the efforts of each branch are shared by another branch. When there are compressive forces exerted by the wind, for example, on one part of the building, those are taken again in traction by a structural root. The fact that the roots make contact with the ground ensures the wind-bracing of the unit.

1

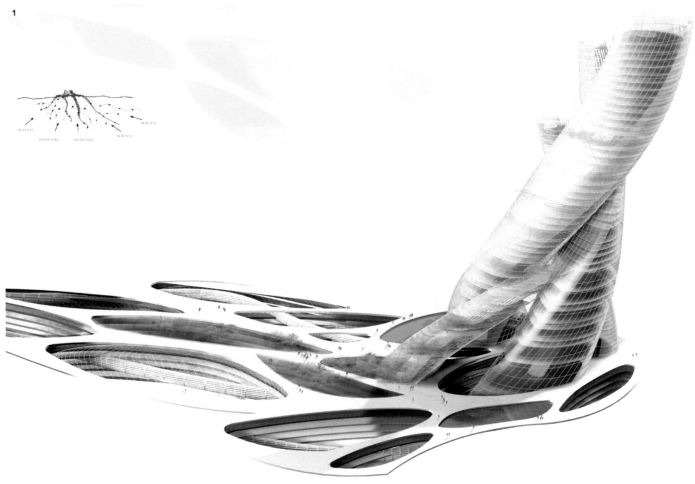

1 Public areas and tower

>SPACESCRAPER
A Manifold Infrastructure for the Exo-urban Condition

Richard Porter, Chris Allen
Cam Helland, Stephen Phillips
United States

Spacescraper creatively invents a new speculative world structure with advanced NASA technology that expands urbanity into outer space. Innovative photovoltaic elevators, powered by lasers, carbon nanotube fiber structures, and advanced environmental control systems, support an extensive universal cable system that houses societal needs on mass scale. Space for individuals, corporations, and entire cities grow to organize within Spacescraper's continuous exoskeletal form. Derived through a series of digital scripting explorations initiated alongside study of carbon molecular structures, Spacescraper performs as a habitable biomimetic network tethering the Earth's atmosphere.

As skyscrapers are historically governed by vertical transport systems (elevators), structural materials (steel) and environmental controls (heat and air-conditioning), Spacescraper proposes to exploit Director Bradley C. Edwards' study at the Institute of Scientific Research for an innovative "space elevator" system. Edwards supposed scientifically that a structural tether could be extended in tension from a satellite (or a meteor) set with a center of mass at geostationary orbit (GEO), 35, 786 km–high above the Earth's surface. Positioned at GEO, gravity does not affect the satellite supporting the tether, and as the tether extends from the equator, it is least susceptible to high winds.

.

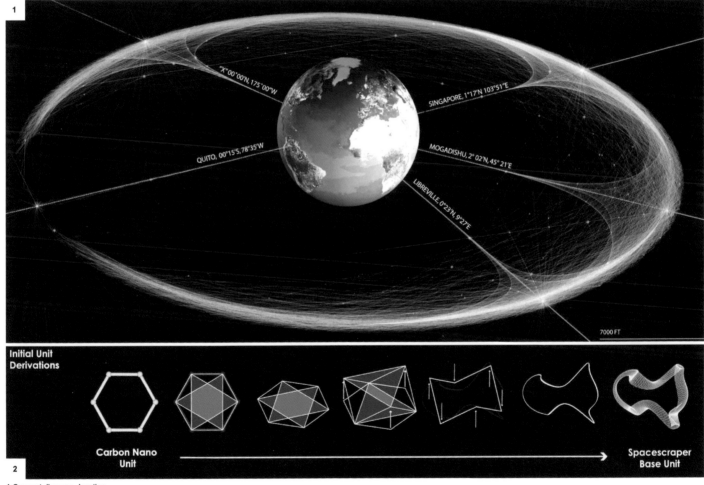

1 Concept diagram - location
2 Geometric unit

In consultation with astro-physicists at Caltech, Spacescraper elaborates Edwards' vision to propose a complex tethering system that uses lightweight carbon nanotube fibers weaved together with structural truss patterns similar to those formed by porifera (sponges). Pre-tensioning the carbon nanotube tethers against the rotation of the Earth increases cable strength, and by adding a series of smaller tethers held-up in tension to numerous satellites positioned at GEO, Spacescraper's extraterrestrial infrastructure achieves equilibrium.

Suspending a futuristic "City-in-Space", Spacescraper naturally grows over time from individual satellite cities to encircle the Earth like a gaseous Saturnine ring. Base towers extend into orbit from several locations along the equator to create a vast series of redundant arteries and nodal support systems. Vital transport consists of local elevators with mass transit lines and hubs that run throughout the orbital network connecting multiple metropolises. Within the twisting overlapped spaces of its complex vertical sections, Spacescraper provides for multiplicity as a new exo-urban megalopolis emerges to innervate outer space as prosthesis to our inevitable posthuman condition.

Spacescraper was formed through mutual collaboration between Stephen Phillips of Stephen Phillips Architects (SPARCHS) and recent Cal Poly architecture graduates and design interns Chris Allen, Cameron Helland, and Richard Porter.

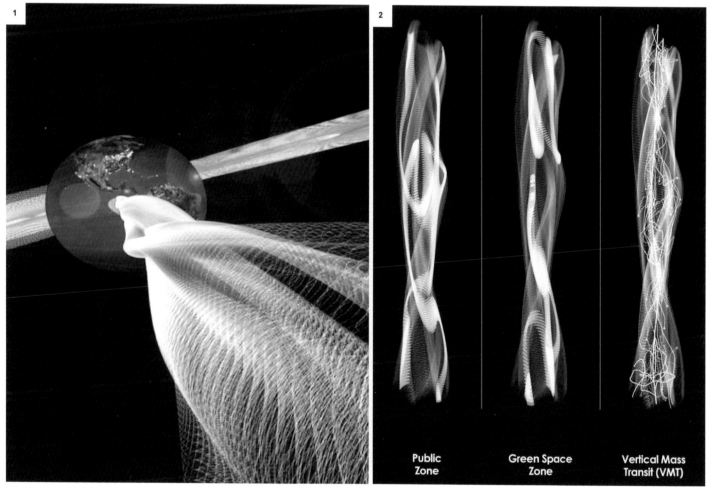

Public Zone   **Green Space Zone**   **Vertical Mass Transit (VMT)**

1 Spacescraper
2 Infrastructure

Jakub Klaska
Czech Republic

This project focuses on the fact that a skyscraper is capable of becoming a landmark within the context of almost every European city. The project Urban Image is based upon the potential of the skyscraper to become the landmark of a particular area. Every megastructure in Holland is a highly planned act with strictly defined regulations. The extreme lack of space in cities such as Amsterdam doesn't allow mega-developments, as seen in Asia nowadays, or in the USA through the XX Century.

The site is located within a very thin and long urban strip which is bound by the river to the north side and by the railway tracks to the south. These two elements open the space on each side of the strip. This open and unbuilt area gives space to fully perceive the Urban Image. Urban Image, as the landmark of the whole area, concentrates the energy in order to redistribute it back to the city. It functions as a landmark to the mood of the place, culture, tradition and spatial context of the area. The shape of generic tower skyscrapers is to be redefined within such context. Verticality should be used as a tool to design a skyscraper as a landmark. The huge mass of generic tower skyscrapers is unwrapped, becoming a very thin slab; this makes internal life visible, and brings the interior closer to the outside.

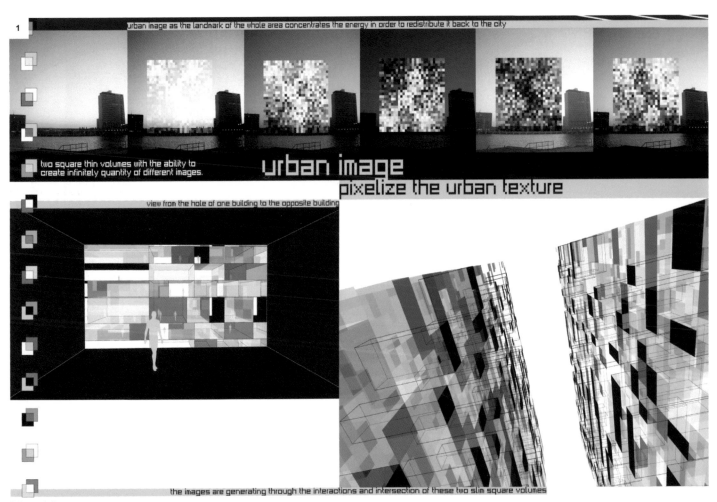

1 Concept diagrams

Urban Image consists of two very thin square shaped slabs which accommodate different programs. The square shape provides a legible frame. The image is being generated through the interactions and visible intersections of these two slabs, according to light or darkness, and the different use of the multi-purpose buildings at any given time. It becomes a scene you can peep into. The slab is doubled in order to create more variations, to make the scenographic intention visible and to bring certain enjoyment from the interaction and tension between the slabs.

The inner spaces of the thin slabs support the creation of the image through different concentration of mass according to the purpose of each space. There are many different degrees of transparency and concentration of mass within the slabs. The most transparent parts of the building are holes and the others vary in different degrees concentration of mass according to their function. There are two basic types of holes. The first type is being generated by inter-sections of different programs within the buildings. These holes are collective open spaces for intersected programs. The second type consists of private open-air spaces within sections of the buildings.

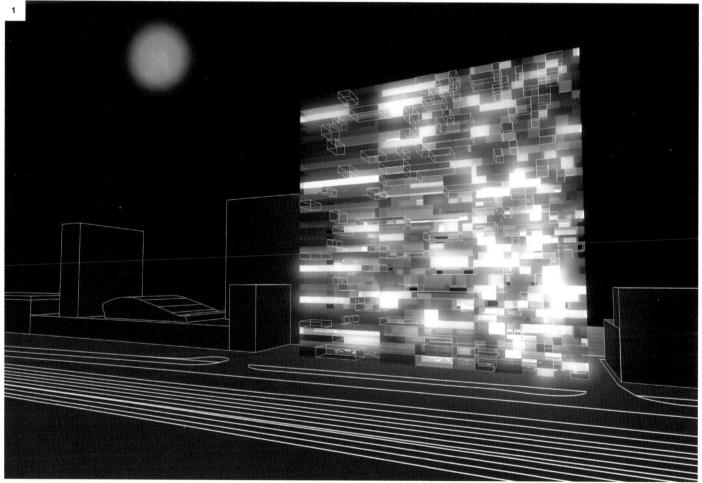

1 Street view

eVolo

08 SKYSCRAPER COMPETITION

This is a proposal for a 720m tall skyscraper to be located above the existing Belarussky Train Station in Moscow, Russia. The program consists of a hotel, assembly, retail, cultural spaces, and apartments. These respond to the needs of the site, which serves as a major gateway to Moscow by road and rail. The main road to St. Petersburg runs through the site and is intersected by the main train line to Europe. Built in 1870, Belarussky Train Station is one of Moscow's most important historical structures. It was celebrated throughout its history and earned the moniker 'victory station' for its role in shuttling Soviet troops to the German front during WWII, and for receiving the first trainloads of soldiers returning victorious after the war.

The process of designing a skyscraper for this site faced two problems above and beyond the issues typically confronted by skyscrapers, built above complex interchanges of roads, rails, and subways. Firstly, the building needed to address multiple urban contexts which varied drastically in their history, form, and program. Secondly, the design needed to confront the environmental difficulties of building in Moscow's harsh climate. The solution proposes to de-laminate the performative layers necessary for skyscraper construction (structure, weatherized enclosure, solar control, circulation, and mechanical systems), in order to solve these divergent problems. The de-laminated layers are programmed with technical functions and then interwoven amongst each other. Most spatial conditions are defined as the spaces between (and serviced by) these layers, but at key juncture points (programmatically and structurally) the layers interweave forming more complex spaces.

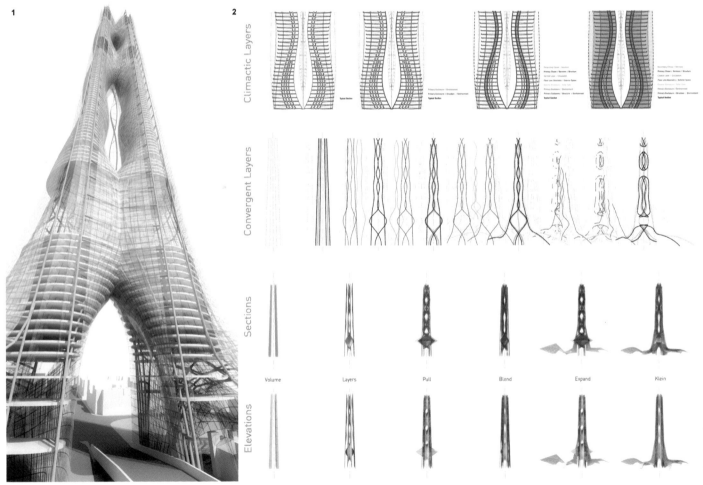

1 Street view
2 Concept diagrams

Urbanistically, the de-laminated layers 'interiorize' the existing urban context within multiple levels of spatial enclosure. As the building approaches the ground, it splits to form a literal gateway over the city's main street. At the same time, several of the layers pass over Belarussky Station to form a glass canopy above the tracks, while also helping to preserve the existing building. Other layers pass over the existing 'object building' modern context elsewhere in the site, turning the otherwise useless expanses of open space between those buildings into partially weatherized, and thus usable, public space.

Ecologically, the de-laminated layers allow for the 'interiorization' of multiple climactic zones. Each of the layers traps a zone of passively conditioned air. Each progressive layer of air insulates the layers within, meaning each layer takes progressively less energy to heat or cool. During the winter, the outer layers function as greenhouses, heating the inner ones. During the summer, the heat generated by the outer layers generates a stack effect – the rapidly rising air aids in passive ventilation and cooling. As a result, the building responds sectionally to its climate. During times of extreme cold and heat, the inhabitants of the skyscraper can withdraw into the inner layers, while at other times they can freely use the interstitial spaces between the layers. For special needs, each hotel or apartment occupant can choose, as required, to expend the extra energy needed to condition their share of the interstitial spaces, meaning that their domesticated space can 'expand' or 'contract' as they need as well.

1
2

1 Aerial view
2 Perspectives

Rugel Chiriboga, Ted Givens
United States

Our project is based in Jurong East, Singapore. The site benefits from its adjacency to a mass transit line station and beautiful natural lake amenity. It is located between a Chinese garden and a heavy industrial district with large residential developments. Unfortunately, these residential developments do not take full advantage of sustainable building opportunities that are inherent in this region. Cultural richness and diversity in use, sustainability, and innovation particular to climatic influences in the region were primary drivers for our concept development. Our intent is to blend site specific sustainable strategies with a new interpretation of high rise design, derived from the juxtaposition of the vibrant complexity found in the traditional Malay village and the streamlined efficiency of modern Singapore. We sought clues from nature that could be utilized to develop a sustainable approach that would provide a stark contrast to the existing architectural landscape. The heavy use of gardens, both in the landscape and in the towers, provides a point of cultural departure in a sea of relentless housing blocks adjacent to our site.

An interesting fact about Singapore is that amidst constant deluges, Singapore has to buy its fresh water from Malaysia, due to a lack of adequate reservoirs. Water conservation thus became a primary initiative in concept development. In formulating a response to this challenge, we gained inspiration from the Wah Kim orchid, the national flower that pulls water directly from the air. There is inherent beauty in its form, and efficiency in the manner by which the orchid draws sustenance from its environment. This flower became a wonderful source of inspiration in developing a sustainable strategy for our mixed-use hotel and residential towers. The organic form of our buildings jumps out into the air to catch falling rain water.

1

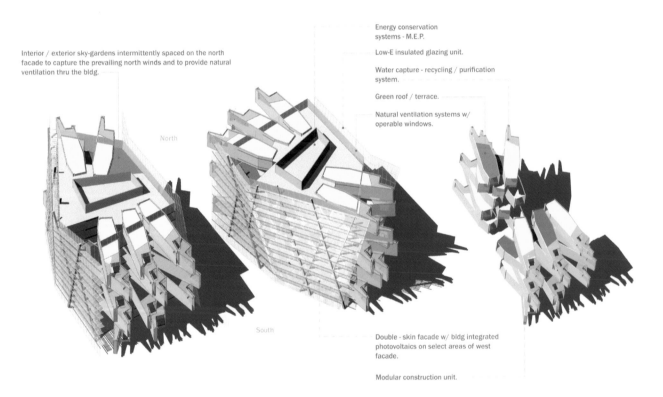

Interior / exterior sky-gardens intermittently spaced on the north facade to capture the prevailing north winds and to provide natural ventilation thru the bldg.

North

South

Energy conservation systems - M.E.P.

Low-E insulated glazing unit.

Water capture - recycling / purification system.

Green roof / terrace.

Natural ventilation systems w/ operable windows.

Double - skin facade w/ bldg integrated photovoltaics on select areas of west facade.

Modular construction unit.

Sustainable Strategies:

There is inherent beauty in its form, and efficiency in the manner by which the orchid draws sustenance from its environment. This is a wonderful source of inspiration in continuing to develop a sustainable strategy for our mixed-use hotel and residential towers in Singapore.

1 Program, concept diagram

With this as our starting point, the sustainable strategy for the towers became locally referential and provided for an environmentally inspired cooling and ventilation approach. The tower placements capitalize on the prevailing north winds to provide through ventilation in the buildings. The roofs of the modular pod units oriented to the north and south for the residences utilize a water-reclamation system to capture rainwater, purify it, and use it for cooling and gray water use. Energy for the system is generated by the building integrated photovoltaic cells in the double skin glass façade on the west face of the towers, where the majority of the solar radiation in Singapore occurs throughout the year.

Most of the modular residential pods have a green roof to assist with cooling and terraces for the residents' use. The configuration of the pods for the north and south facades create dynamic exterior and interior sky gardens, capitalizing on climatic influences. The resulting undulations and overhangs formed by the placement of the units provide shade for the south facades. The units also peek out around the side skins to catch glimpses of an adjacent Chinese garden, lake, and newly created public area at the base of the towers. Connections to the community and site are established immediately upon arrival at various levels. The new public park and arrival plaza connect the hotel and residential towers to the community via natural landscape, orchid gardens, and undulating green roof areas, which conceal parking below.

1 Housing units
2 Elevation, diagrams

>COASTAL FOG TOWER

Alberto Fernández, Susana Ortega
Chile

Huasco City is a port in the north of Chile. The city is a place of important agricultural development thanks to the Huasco River, but in the last decade the water flux decreased, which will probably lead to agriculture disappearance in the near future. A new strategy is required to obtain water from the Atacama Desert. In this place there is a climatic phenomenon called Camanchaca, dense coastal fog that has dynamic characteristic: condensation at great heights that is carried towards coastal zones by strong wind currents. Its origin is in the anticyclone of the Pacific Ocean that produces a layer of stratocumulus, covering the coastal strip from Peru to northern Chile. The base of the cloud is at 400 meters (with a variation of 200 meters) above sea level. The second layer contains minerals from the sea, in lower concentration than sea water.

The idea is to build towers that collect water from these clouds and provide it to new agricultural land along the coast. The towers are 400 meters-high, and designed to catch water particles in the air that come from the coast to the Valley of the Huasco River. The anticipated performance, ranges from two to ten liters per square meter of vertical surface. Each tower has 10,000 square meters of vertical surface, producing a minimum of 20,000 liters per day, and an impressive maximum of 100,000 liters. There will be enough water to start agriculture in this arid coastal region.

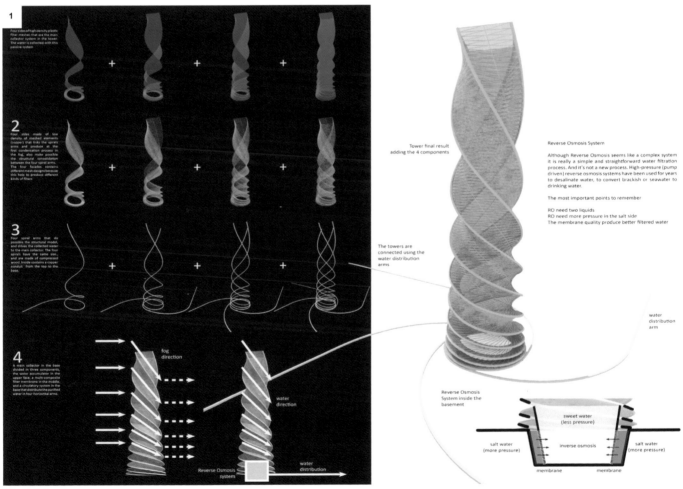

1 Concept diagrams

The tower is composed of four components with specific functions:

1. Four sides of high density plastic meshes that serve as water collectors.

2. Four sides of low density meshes (copper) that link the spiral arms.

3. Four spiral arms that serve as structure and transport the collected water into the main cistern.

4. A main cistern located in the base and divided in three parts: a water accumulator in the upper face, a multi-composite filter membrane in the middle, and a circulatory system that distributes the purified water.

1   2

1 Perspective
2 Tower skin

The Freeway Interchange Tower seeks to reclaim the "throw-away" land often left in the wake of massive highway junctions, typically an abandoned, unattractive space at the center of maze-like crossings. These infrastructure nexus not only serve as transportation nodes, but also act as buffers between differing land conditions, uses, and city environments. In this particular site, the freeway interchange is bordered by low density residential neighborhoods on the south and east sides, a nearby institutional center to the north, and a major drainage canal to the northwest. With such proximity to varying uses and zoning regions, the interchange often becomes the separating barrier.

The intent of this proposal is to elevate the status of the interchange from utilitarian infrastructure to one of regional unifier. By sucking up the visual language of southern California's formidable freeway system and coalescing it into an iconic high-rise, the tower can act as a symbolic ribbon that ties the area together, signifying the crossing points of the cities of Anaheim, Orange and Santa Ana. The mixed-use program of the tower - retail, commercial office and high end hotel near the top - completes the micro-arcology of the area, complementing existing nearby residential and recreational uses. At the same time, the tower reinforces the Southern California automotive culture, celebrating the constant dynamism and technological achievement of its impressive freeway system.

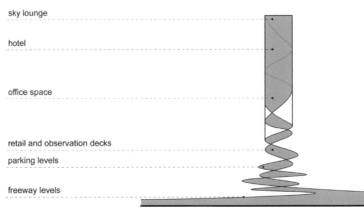

sky lounge

hotel

office space

retail and observation decks

parking levels

freeway levels

1 Location, program diagram
2 Aerial view
3 Street view

In a vision for the future of the these endless sprawl zones so ubiquitous to southern California, Interchange Tower would be the common place connecting and completing the local ecosystems. With the development of "community towers", destination nodes would be created that enhance local economic stability (retail), relocate and diversify commercial office space, as well as form areas of vertical social density encompassing high end hotels and condominiums. Ironically, the Interchange Tower would serve to reduce the burden of excessive automobile transportation by creating waypoints; however, this intervention would also begin to render the mega interchange (its habitat) obsolete with the reduced need for such infrastructure.

In conceiving the idea of the Interchange Tower the parti was developed in which the freeway strata was brought quite literally into the tower, forming a symbiotic relationship between site context and object. As the automobiles are brought into the building, they would circulate up to the parking levels which are followed by retail and observation decks, office space, hotel, and final a sky lounge. In order to create a unified language based on the sweeping lines of the freeway below, the tower's outer skin is composed of a helical ribbon of aluminum panels which serve two main functions; first and foremost a sound damping system to control the noise inherent of its surroundings, and secondly as a sun shading device which is more sinuous at the lower levels to allow more or less light at the upper levels, where solar shading is necessary.

1

2

1 Elevation
2 Highway view

>SYMBIOTIC INTERLOCK

Daekwon Park
United States

Skyscrapers started to emerge in cities like Chicago and New York towards the end of 19th Century. Over a century has passed, and the skyscrapers become the norm for the big city centers throughout the world. Although the skyscraper itself is truly an achievement of modern technology and vision, the urban space that is created by the collection of these seems to be fragmented, limited, and very unkind to nature. The project takes place in this urban context, investigating the way to reunite the isolated city blocks and insert a multi-layered network of public space, green space, and nodes for the city.

Structure + Core
The main structure of this facility consists of two components. The first is the core, which acts as a spine for the units to be plugged into, and the second is the interlocking structure which distributes the overall load of the tower to the surface, slab, and the main structure of the existing skyscraper.

Wind Turbine Unit
This unit is designed to incorporate four wind turbines which convert the kinetic energy of the wind that flows through the skyscrapers into electrical energy. Vertical-axis wind turbine among the various types of wind turbine is chosen due to its flexibility in locating the generator and the efficiency in utilizing the wind energy from both windward and leeward sides.

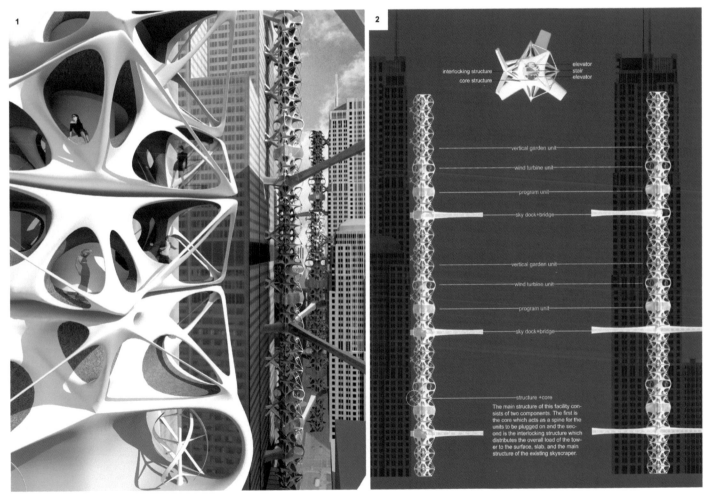

1 Perspective
2 Program diagram

Vertical Garden Unit
The vertical garden unit is an open structure which provides a habitat for plants, insects, and animals, which also becomes a public park for cities where natural spaces are limited. This unit is combined and multiplied throughout the towers in order to achieve positive effects, such as reducing the urban heat and filter pollutants from the air.

Sky Dock + Bridge
The sky dock unit is the node where the network between the towers and the existing skyscrapers takes place. The bridge connects the nodes to create a city where activity, movement, and events occur in multiple layers rather than just on the ground level and inside the skyscrapers.

Program Unit
The program unit is an enclosed space which accommodates multiple functions such as café, meeting room, observatory, museum, information center, retail, game room, restrooms, media library, etc. The program will be determined according to the location and the users of the units.

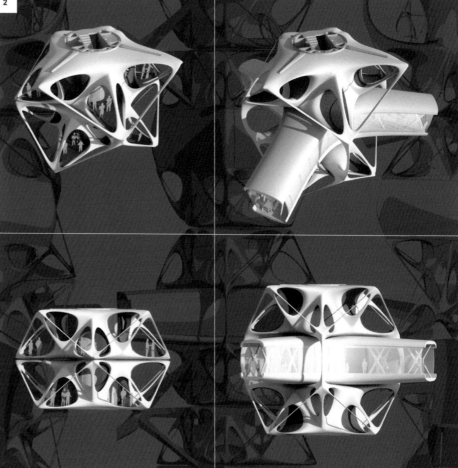

1 Street view
2 Types of units

>INTERACTIVE TRANSITION
A Living - Tower

Tingxing Tao
United States

Interaction is the influence of two systems on one another, which can be understood as interchange and interrelation between the two. Transition means the connection from one status to another, or a gradual or sudden transformation between the two parts. Living-Tower is designed as a vertical strategy that situates itself within the most complex urban context- Shanghai, which is considered as the fastest-developing city in the fastest-developing country. Emphasis of this project is given to examining the idea of the interactive transition within and outside a building.

The theme, interactive transition, emerges when two systems react to each other. First of all, with a flexible-weaving base, the tower is a self-organizing creature, standing above a sophisticated highway joint, not only creating a new relationship between the architecture and the vehicular circulation, but also saving a huge amount of space within the urban area.

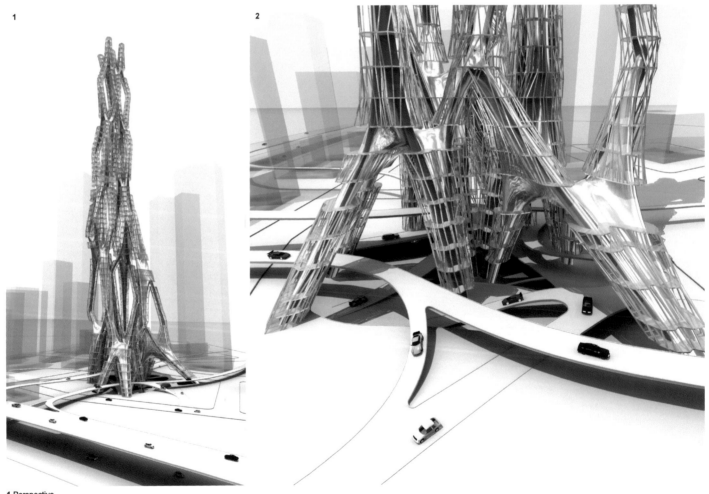

1 Perspective
2 Highway intersection

Interface between Units
Apartments are defined by their users, and the overall shape of the building is a response to these forces. Bridges are the result of reaction between these tubular units. Transition spaces connect different families, different generations, create the possibility of communication within the neighborhood.

Program & Geometry.
We obtained the geometrical results thanks to the analysis of the architectural program.. The building is characterized by nodes which provide space for amenities and public recreation.

Horizontality & Verticality.
At the base of the tower, there is interaction with the environment. The legs of the tower spread out, between the highway. The landscape becomes a mix of horizontality and verticality. A Living-Tower is explicit as a strategy towards a progressive building prototype idea, seeking a dialogue between the rapidly transforming city and its inhabitants. Architecture itself becomes an infinite feedback loop into the future.

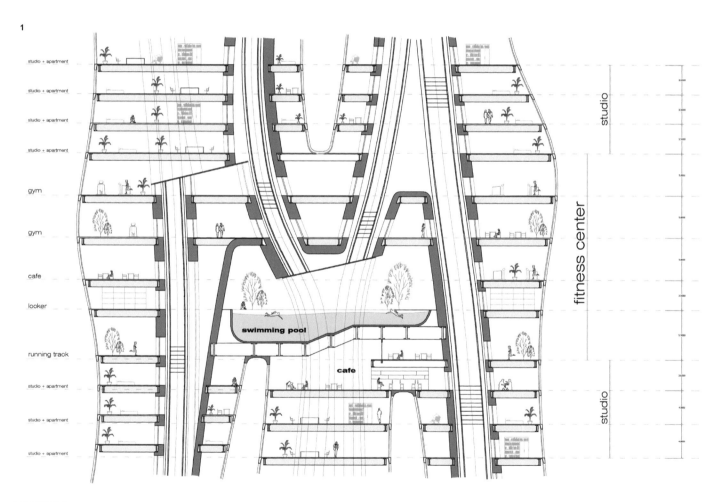

1 Cross section

Ben Simmons, Daniel O. Ware
Ginger Watkins, Joseph H. Tiu
United States

V-Hive for Vertical Hive - a concept for skyscraper design utilizing the natural organic growth of unitary hexagonal cells, which cluster, grow, and evolve to form honeycomb colonies in a vertical fashion, and applied to the vertical nature of skyscrapers. By creating a lattice structure to which these cells can attach, the organic germinating nature of city growth is reproduced. The clustering of individual cells form sky-pod colonies, which themselves become "neighborhoods" or "buildings", in a vertical urban environment. Thus the life and energy of the two-dimensional/horizontal urban fabric of the city is continued along on the three-dimensional/vertical axis through the void/core of a transparent and environmentally permeable structure. This allows for the formation of an open-air 360 degree vertical urban corridor. This concept takes skyscraper design from the vacuum of visual icon to the experiential level of the vertical street. The honeycomb is the most efficient geometric structure in terms of using the least amount of material needed to obtain stability. Modular and rigorously structured, yet evolves into an organic whole.

Circulation. This public transportation system is engineered to transition from underground, to a vertical orientation. This alleviates the need to stop, find parking and/or change into the secondary mode of vertical transportation such as elevators. All other infrastructure is designed to "seamlessly" transition from a horizontal into a vertical system.

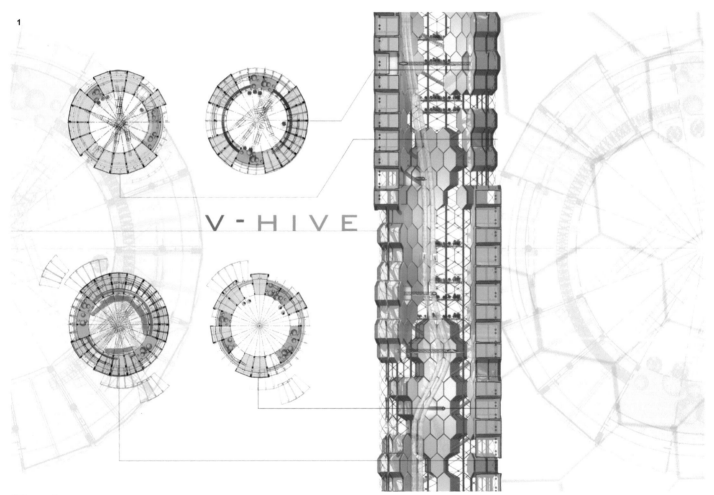

1

1 Plans, section

Community. The lattice structure which is open, is transformed to form the "plazas" and "side streets" where communities can interact as well as provide open-air circulation between the sky-pod colonies. This also brings "to light" the isolated nature of city dwelling in typical buildings, in which individual levels do not interact with one another. By providing the visually apparent nature of an open vertical urban core within the skyscraper, community identity (hive) is reinforced.

Optimization. Just as a plant thrives in its own particular niche, different building types will colonize the facets of the V-HIVE according to their needs. Residences, with higher heating needs, face southward, as offices, with demand for even light and lower cooling loads, tend to the North. As a self-sustaining colony, every liability becomes an asset, every waste, reused. The district systems serve to balance any excess that optimal orientation and passive systems cannot.

Adaptation. Growing and evolving, each individual can take advantage of the unique niches of vertical real estate created in the hive. At a scale accessible to the individual vertical farmer, shoe shiner, or attorney, the lattice provides framework which can support the smallest entrepreneur or largest corporate entity.

1 Infrastructure

>INCOMPLETE MONUMENT
A Decomposing Embassy

Frank Mahan
United States

The government-established program for the new U.S. embassy currently under construction in Baghdad is extraordinarily large, dwarfing any other embassy in the world.

This project accepts this dubious program as its starting point, but questions how it and the architecture might change over time. In the first radical gesture, the embassy is configured as a tower, the most iconic, visible, and counterintuitive form for the building.

Next, to advance the architectural project and test one possible scenario for the embassy's decomposition, a hypothetical timeline for U.S. withdrawal based on an optimistic assumption of gradual but continuous improvement is proposed.

Finally, as the political, economic, and security situations improve in Iraq, programmatic units of the building are removed, gradually creating an incomplete monument to this challenging period. The U.S. withdrawal is registered by the form of the building.

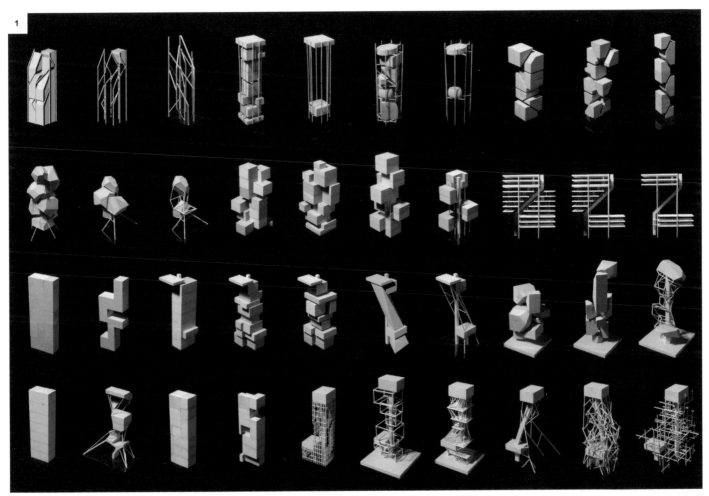

1 Study models

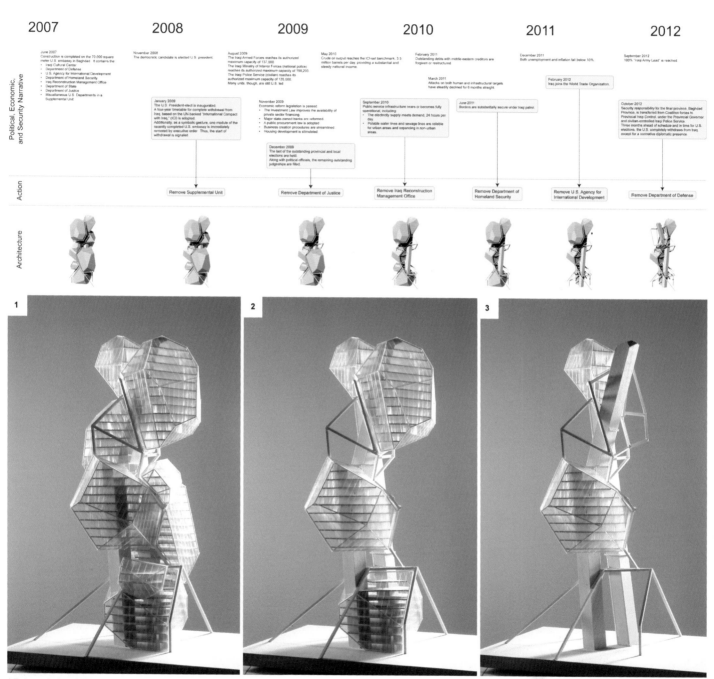

2007   **2008**   **2009**   **2010**   **2011**   **2012**

1 Embassy in June 2007
2 Embassy in June 2011
3 Embassy in October 2012

>VIRTUAL TOWERS

Vincent Barué
France

Live in a tower if you want to! Simply push one button to look beyond the horizon, watch the sun rising, admire your town's aerial view. See without being seen with a complete view range of 360 degrees. Live the tower without the disadvantages, the price, the fears and dangers.

Plugged in the city, the virtual towers are integrated in difficult landscapes and urban fabrics, without constituting a mask for the buildings neighborhood and the roadway systems. Fine and svelte, they are almost imperceptible and do not fear the bad weather. Structurally, the virtual towers make use of the innumerable court yards of buildings as potential supports. These "urban periscopes" drawn up above the obstacles, offer the inhabitants a dominant panoramic sight of their city and their district, a pricey and rare privilege. Heights are variable and adapted to each place, the towers support chains of cameras laid out to sweep 360°. These new eyes of the neighborhoods exist as virtual windows.

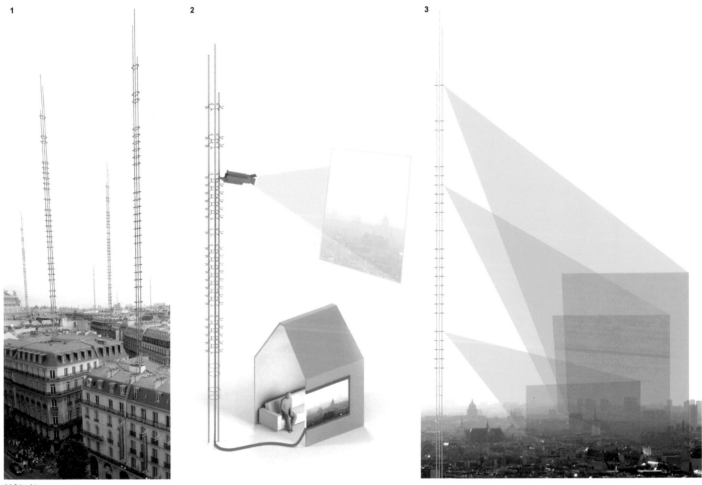

1 Virtual tower cameras
2 Concept diagram
3 Infinite views

The townsmen wishing to benefit from it , chose the orientation and the height of their apartment view. Indeed, each one of their windows can be replaced by a LED screen reconstituting the field of view of one of many cameras.

These "LED window screens" restore a quasi real and psychologically beneficial luminosity for the individuals. The height of the cameras guaranteed to benefit from the solar luminosity, from dusk until dawn. Moreover, LED are ecological and affordable because they diffuse neither UV nor infra-reds and can be recycled to 98 percent. Their energy consumption is minimal and they have exceptional life-span.

This concept of "virtual towers" can obviously be applied to a wide variety of scenarios, which would benefit from the feeling of freedom that comes with the new view.

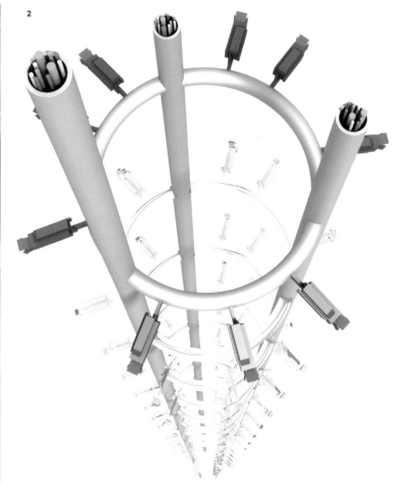

1 Before and after views of an apartment
2 Virtual tower infrastructure

Paral.lel.

Paral.lel is the result of the modeling of the skyscraper's archetype. Several parallelepipeds are transformed following different directions. This design, obtained through three different "formal actions" (stretch, bend, wrap), brings a new perspective to the skyscraper's usual design; the building is perceived differently from different points in the city. Size and height are not important. What is crucial is the relation between skyscraper's design and its position in the city (at urban and human scale).

Interiors / exteriors.

The kyscraper interiors are made of wide glass partition with breathtaking views of the urban skyline. The partitions are design with a solid texture of alveolar plot, so that interiors are filled with daylight, whether its a business or residential space. Exterior texture is the same on all sides of the skyscraper. A particular torsion makes every sides bend towards every direction in space. This unique structure makes Paral.lel a creative process that can be applied to any building. Paral.lel is not a simple aesthetic form of urban design.

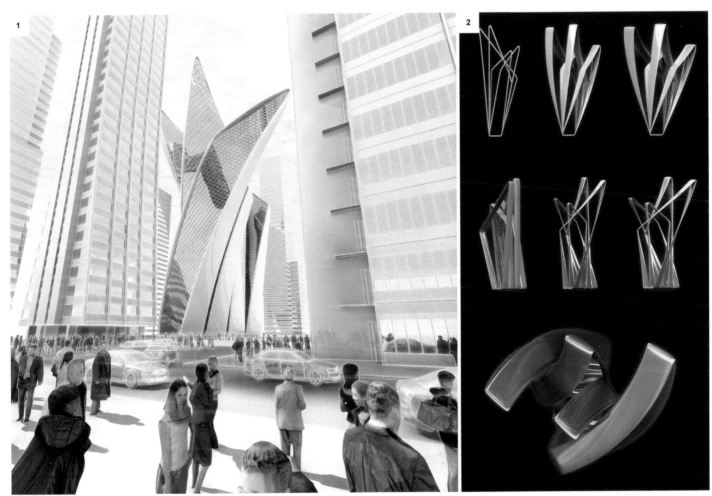

1 View from street
2 Concept diagram

1 Aerial view
2 Interior

Min Ter Lim
United States

The world needs the skyscraper. The continuous growth in population demands a strategy for vertical density with diverse programmatic types. We are already witnessing the proliferation, almost at a fanatic rate, of skyscrapers worldwide. Mixed-use developments have been evolving through the last decade and today these mega-structures are becoming autonomous cities.

We should not look at them as objects from the last century, but as an ever changing response to our needs. In fact, the future of the skyscraper described by countless futurists and utopians is today at hand. Skyscrapers have become containers of worlds, in which each world is independent from the others. The future lies in our ability to pack all our needs (housing, offices, leisure, education, and recreational areas) in one vertical structure.

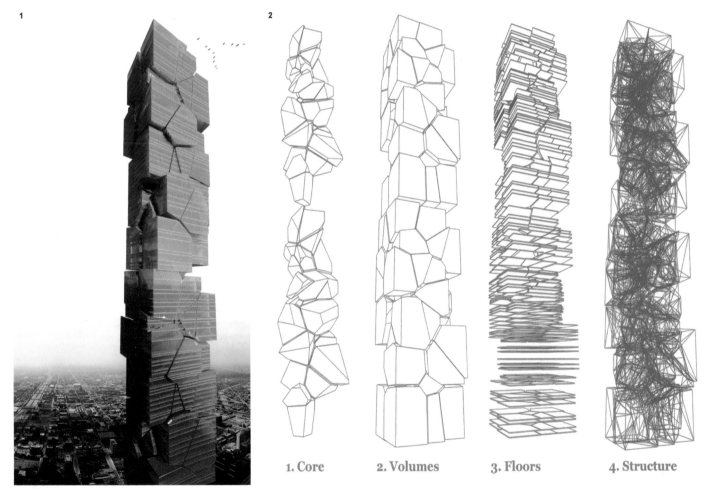

1. Core   2. Volumes   3. Floors   4. Structure

1 Aerial view
2 Concept diagrams

1 View from terraces
2 Skin
3 Street view

Daniel Hammerman, Kevin Kehler
United States

Inspired by the transformative process of rusting and ecological gradients of day lighting, our mixed-use tower twists and modulates from a thin, flaky character to a sharp, solid condition as it rises from Battery Park City, in Lower Manhattan. Facade porosity varies in response to environmental simulations and incident solar calculations, becoming more open on the north face, while more enclosed on other elevations, and distribution of program is informed by interior day lighting levels. The concrete core, composite slab and complex lateral bracing are clad in Corian panels, which have been thoroughly studied for curvature and seaming to delineate and accentuate continuity of flow from floor to wall to window mullions to ceiling.

We have developed and deployed innovative digital techniques in an opportunistic fashion for the generation of growth and evaluation of patterns in the emergence of form which is greater than the sum of its parts, yet manifest at every scale from birds-eye to detail. Elegant organizations are highly integrated formal/spatial systems which operate similar to organic systems. Form results from adaptation to performance requirements and the holistic integration of structure, circulation, and skin, imbued with an intelligence of fabrication and assembly. Precise geometry and high-order surface continuity inform the continuous differentiation of our skyscraper.

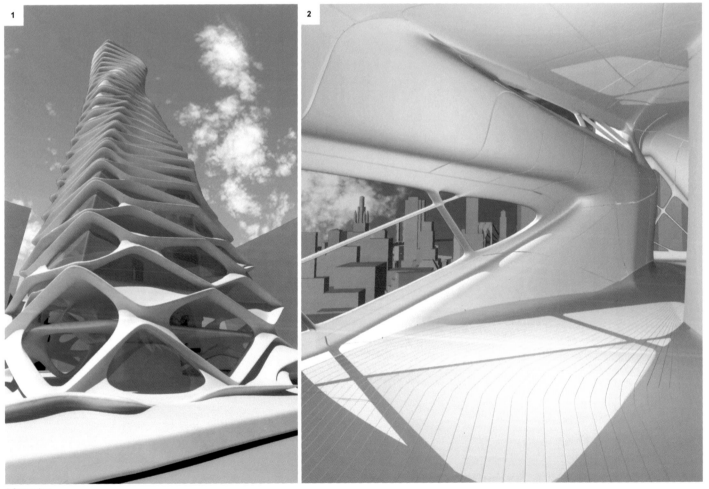

1 Street view
2 Apartment

1

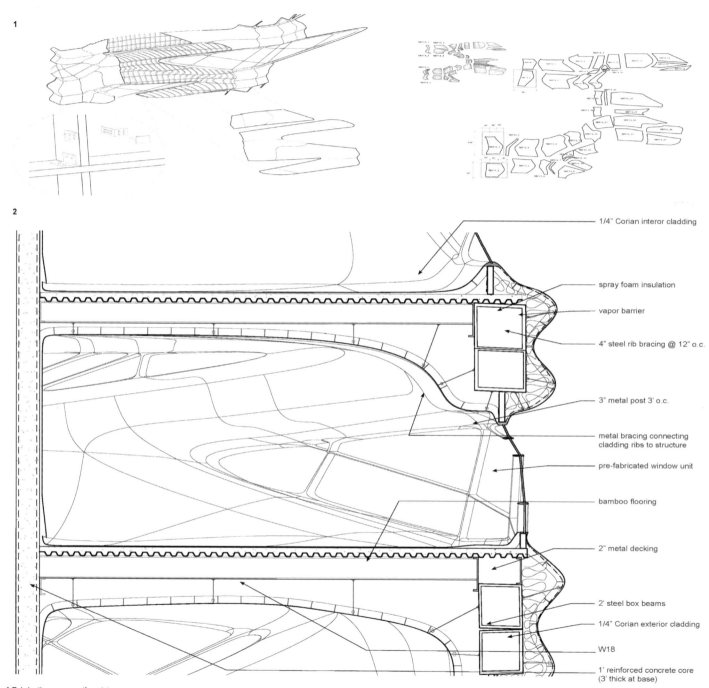

2

1/4" Corian interior cladding

spray foam insulation

vapor barrier

4" steel rib bracing @ 12" o.c.

3" metal post 3' o.c.

metal bracing connecting
cladding ribs to structure

pre-fabricated window unit

bamboo flooring

2" metal decking

2' steel box beams

1/4" Corian exterior cladding

W18

1' reinforced concrete core
(3' thick at base)

1 Fabrication process (facade)
2 Facade detail

The ground represents everyday affairs, such as people, politics, traffic, pollution. We work and live on the ground, shuffle through corridors, wait on roads, and it is still on the surface where our life takes place. The sky is freedom, heaven, a place to dream, wish, and escape. To escape from everything on the ground, we have to climb into the sky. Conventional skyscrapers allow us to elevate ourselves and gaze out over the city, but the feeling of being separated and enclosed remains. The dialogue is one-way; we cannot interact with or enter the sky. We are like animals behind a glass, unable to break free from the world below.

Escaper is an instrument to catch the sky. It avoids direct visual contact with the ground by twisting its body. Its reflective skin presents an image of the upper atmosphere. Escaper wraps and folds around itself, allowing the sky to be part of the building, and the building a part of the sky. By making itself an element of the firmament, it eludes the eyes on the ground, despite its massive volume. It is made from three buildings, which intertwine to create a shifting dynamic between volumes, functions, and people. Between the three connected volumes, the sky is contained in a central space, punctuated by large floating gardens. Three vertical cores run through the gardens, allowing people to ascend directly to and between them. The five strata of artificial ground inhabit the sky and are meeting and gathering spaces for people from the three volumes. They are for everybody, a congregation above the city.

1

2

garden (every floor)

artificial ground

1 Perspective
2 Sky gardens, terraces

The three dividing and converging buildings that comprise Escaper vary from one another in function and character. By connecting these buildings to each other by means of the large artificial gardens, these functions and characters can merge, activities can mix and finally inspire a new movement in the sky. In a conventional skyscraper, all functions are piled vertically, stacking up on each other to the point where we can rarely understand the many different activities on the other floors. We may be vertically just a few meters away from a situation that we are completely unable to comprehend. It is an insular approach, sealing people into their compartment and not allowing interaction or cross-fertilization. With this method of juxtaposition we can rarely gain new experiences, and it leads to the monotonous repetition of everyday tasks. It serves only to make a dull, depressing and inhumane life for the people in the building.

Escaper seals itself from the ground, but opens itself to the sky. In the captured section of the atmosphere, Escaper mixes and merges function, activity, context, and life, to create a rich canopy of happenings. The structure promotes communication and interaction, while simultaneously supporting private, intimate spaces that can be used for personal reflection or private encounters. The dialogue is between people, sky and volumes, and these are detached from and unknown to the world below.

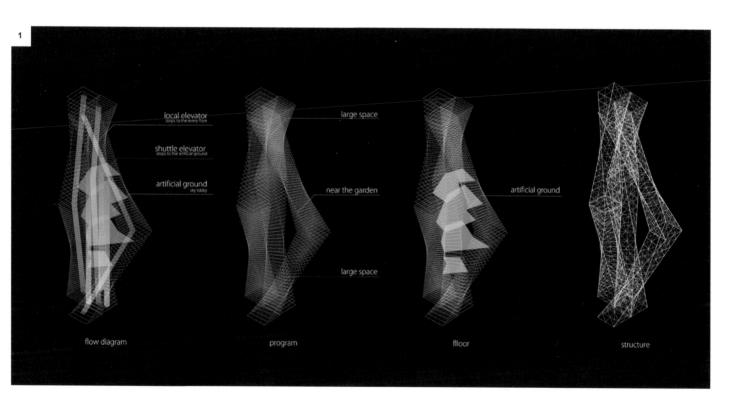

1 Concept diagrams

**Claudiu Barsan-Pipu, Oana Maria Nituica
Irina Maria Dragomir, Bogdan Nicolae Ispas**
Romania

The "genetic" predisposition

The urban structure of the city of Bucharest was designed without a master plan; since its creation, drifting neighborhoods developing around religious centers have defined its urban characteristics. This continuous migration, as well as the poor "circulatory irrigation", led to a city predisposed to suffer from massive "urban strokes", both in terms of functional disposition, as well as in the associated circulatory system.

The stroke

During the last years of the communist regime, Ceausescu tried to impose his utopist, totalitarian vision over Bucharest. His top-bottom approach did not manage to change the urban structure of the city, but merely cause a massive stroke in its continuity. By the significant intervention, that eradicated almost a quarter of the old urban tissue in his attempt to "upgrade" the city, he only created the premises for what was about to be known as urban necrosis.

Urban necrosis

As it is often the case after a major, near fatal stroke, the urban tissue of Bucharest was severely affected by the urban stroke Ceausescu induced. The necrosis of the "new urbanisim" led to an increasing separation from the rest of the city in terms of public appeal and commercial functions.

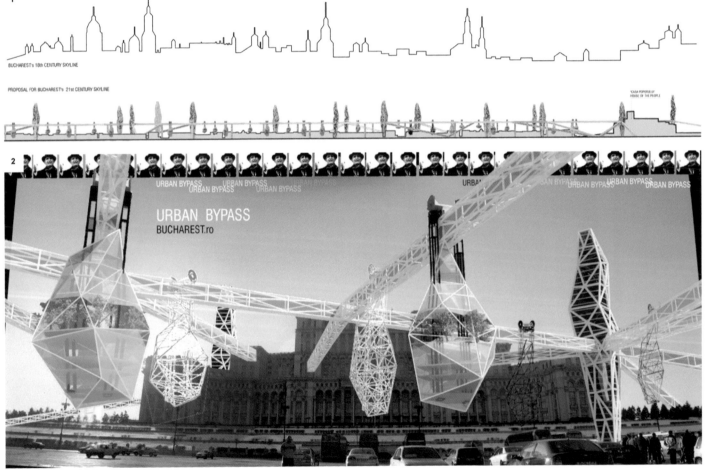

1 Bucharest before and after project
2 Urban By-Pass

Urban by-pass

Our proposal tries to suggest a new type of radical intervention, to rise up to the utopist totalitarian urban dream. We propose a vascular urban system that can revitalize the affected tissue and, without any attempt to hide the scars, provide a new start, a new lifestyle, and a new building approach.

As Ceausescu literally erased all the urban structures of a pseudo-rural city; we are now emphasizing two major changes.

1) Restoring the link between the old (traditional tissue) and the new (Communist and contemporary interventions) by recreating a new urban system; overlapping the existing and by-passing the flow of public interest to these dysfunctional spaces.

2) Creating ecological hotspots that can provide a new and self-sufficient way of living, acting and socializing, with continuous interlinks between the one and the many, the small pseudo-rural traditional houses of Bucharest and the gigantic communist spatiality.

1 New Bucharest

Maria Pasavento, Fabio Ferrian
Lara Rizzardini
Italy

MILone is the result of a research begun during the Integrated Design Workshop of Prof. Montuori at IUAV (University Institute of Architecture in Venice).

It is conceived as an outside-in city, located in the near periphery of Milan, and called to be an attraction point of the area, where green, stone paths, wooden relaxation areas and water basins are projected to foster a symbiotic relationship between the natural and the artificial environments.

MILone is to allude to Pirellone, the famous Gio Ponti's tower, symbol of Milan, in the year of the 80th anniversary of the foundation of Domus, by G. P. himself.

MILone is thought to be a "Fuori Salone" area of the Milan's Expos, where art exhibitions, design expos and collateral events could take place. The final conviction is that the building's substance should have environmental qualities that create a state of well-being, making use of tools of architecture that translate into space, materials, and colors.

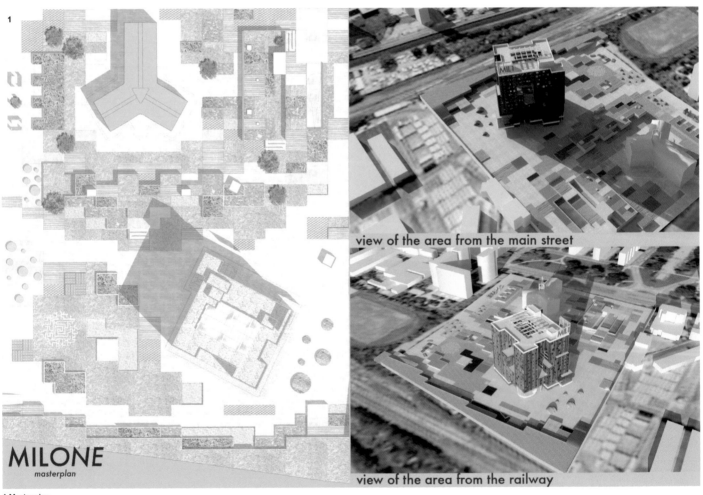

view of the area from the main street

view of the area from the railway

MILONE
masterplan

1 Master plan

1 North elevation
2 South elevation
2 View from plaza

>ESCAPE: A NEW URBAN DIMENSION

Akram Damisi, Ghalia Bisharat, Firas Thalji
Alaa Abdalat, Ashraf Damisi
Jordan

The concept of high density in cities is one that has transformed the modern city. Architecture and technology made the development of towers and skyscrapers just another element of the modern city's urban fabric, casting large shadows on social life, both literally and metaphorically speaking. The changed urban fabric brought with it a change in urban life. In these cities, crowdedness, pollution, traffic, noise, and crime, have become an everyday experience. The private, single-use, outsized skyscraper brought on a hefty impact on city life. The instinct to climb up to some high place, from which you can look down and survey your world, seems to be a fundamental human instinct. However, while the rest of the urban world lay in the horizontal, the vertical presence in the city became a privilege for a few; a private realm that towered over the urban stage of everyday life.

Escape blends the private and public realm into a structure that becomes, in essence, a vertical realization of our horizontal urban fabric. The streetscape is stretched and wrapped around a vertical structure, pumping urban existence and energy into a perpendicular stance. This landmark in the city, becomes a natural part of the topography, which includes a physical climb, giving people the satisfaction of climbing up to a high place from which to look down. Escape takes the idea of high density to a new level. It drives the city into the openness of a high-rise structure with public access and mixed lanes that are continuously in use. Residential, commercial and office use, on the banks of a constant ramp that continues from the city street to reach the top of the structure, gives people the benefits of a human scale interaction within a large scale metropolis.

1

2

1 Perspective
2 Conceptual section

A second street wraps around the structure, at instances, intersecting with the first street. This generates an urban feel that is recognized by the users, and that resembles the successful urban plan of much acclaimed cities. The concept of deterritorialization is new, but new things are certainly not without precedent in our evolution, or we'd have had no evolution. When human beings moved from grunting tribalism to the idea of kingdom & empire the idea was new; when human beings moved from monarchy to democracy the idea was new; and of course the idea of a world without borders and/or governments is new, or fairly new, and inevitable. We are one species. despite the fact we often pretend we are not. Escape is not a building, but our addition to the traditional five elements of urban settings. It is an element that people escape into, where all types of amenities are available (residential, commercial, offices, open public spaces) and fit into an element that creates vertical life with all benefits of the horizontal city.

Escape is open to all people, they can enter anytime, as if they were walking on the streets. Since the building structure is formed from two streets going up and intersecting with one another, the circulation within the building becomes easier, mainly by walking or lifts and escalators. It is accessible to all types of people, to enjoy life, and escape the pollution, crowdedness and aggression of the horizontal city.

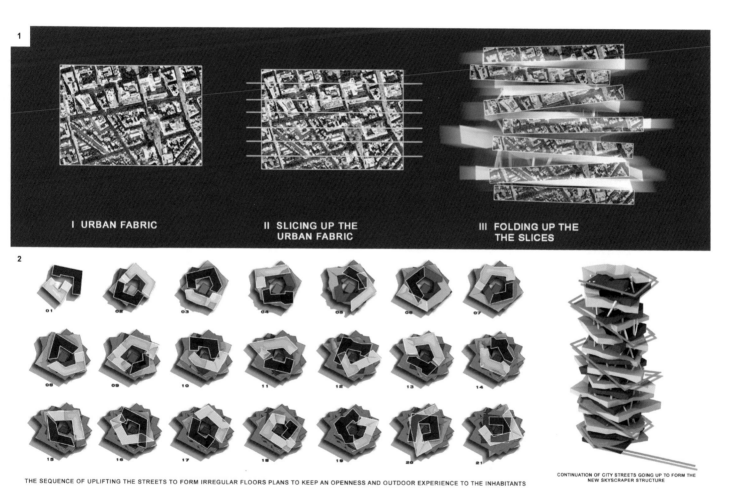

1

I URBAN FABRIC

II SLICING UP THE
URBAN FABRIC

III FOLDING UP THE
THE SLICES

2

THE SEQUENCE OF UPLIFTING THE STREETS TO FORM IRREGULAR FLOORS PLANS TO KEEP AN OPENNESS AND OUTDOOR EXPERIENCE TO THE INHABITANTS

CONTINUATION OF CITY STREETS GOING UP TO FORM THE
NEW SKYSCRAPER STRUCTURE

1 Concept diagrams
2 Access sequence

>FLYSCRAPER

**Paul Burgstaller, Ursula Faix,
Michael Kritzinger**
Switzerland

The 'flyscraper' is a revolutionary and visionary design proposal for the next generation skyscraper, consisting of flying living units, attached with individual 'carbon isogrid'® tubes to the ground. In urban areas across the world we see two phenomena: fast growing metropolitan areas, as well as shrinking cities. The 'flyscraper' is designed for both: deserted as well as congested urban areas. Moreover the 'flyscraper' responds to the existing urban fabric in a very adaptive way, respecting the historical context and heritage landmarks. In addition, the 'flyscraper' offers a solution for very dense urban fabrics, making small, irregularly shaped, and usually commercially worthless pieces of land ('curb property') accessible and worthy for developments; since only ground for the foundation of the 'carbon isogrid'® tubes is needed.

The 'carbon isogrid'® material was originally developed for space research. It is a carbon filament wound structure with shape-memory epoxy which is able to deploy or fold when heated to a prescribed temperature. This allows performing in two ways: first as an overall, stand-alone element, responding to natural heating during daytime (ascending) and natural cooling during night time (descending). The living units, which are also equipped with a helium pad, in order to support the rising of the units, can start to rise with the gaining power of the sun, then slowly descend again after sunset. Secondly, the units are individually controlled by each inhabitant, who can direct them via several shape-memory epoxy "hot spots" on the 'carbon isogrid'® tube from a PC to any desired position.

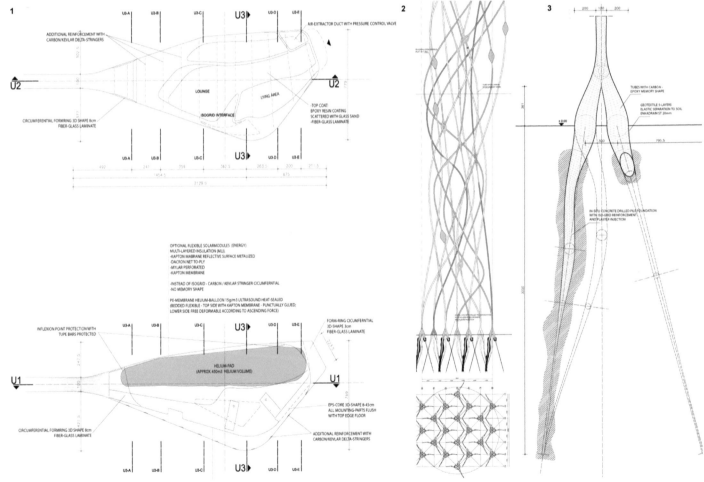

1 Plan and section
2 System section
3 Longitudinal section

The 'isogrid'® tubes are anchored with thee root-like pile-foundations to the ground. In the lower part of the 'flyscraper', special nodes, a widening of a tube, are intentionally interwoven with the 'carbon isogrid'® tubes, so the floating tubes can move elastically and won't mingle accidentally. Therefore, the lower part of the structure forms a very coarsely meshed tissue, which is still navigable. Small helium pads, incorporated to the 'carbon isogrid'® tubes, support the rising of the structure. Past the interwoven part of the structure, the tubes can move individually; crashes are avoided by a security system that keeps units at a certain distance from each other.

The frame of the living unit is made of lightweight fiberglass laminate, reinforced with additional carbon Kevlar delta stringers. The topcoat is made of sand blasted epoxy resin. Each living unit is equipped with a large living area, which is designed in a boomerang shape so living would work for both positions: the flying position and the static position on the ground. Moreover, a kitchen, bathroom, bedroom and the PC control-station are an integral part of the living unit. For environmental reasons, the heating and cooling energy demand of each unit is minimized through multi layer insulation of the living unit's outer skin. The rest of the required energy is generated by ultra-light solar modules, DuPont™ Kapton® polyimide films. Those high-tech solar modules are mounted on the skin of the living unit, exploiting the latest technology in order to maximize their self-sufficiency and sustainability.

1 Perspective of system

>THE URBAN SKI MOUNTAIN

Natalie Ghatan
United Kingdom

The premise behind Urban Mountain is a high-rise geometry that can simultaneously accommodate a vertically-arrayed subsidiary ski community program, along with indoor and outdoor skiing amenities.

The project was informed by examination of the modern city and the phenomena of urban densification, as well as analysis of varied sets of parameters and emergent behaviors. Indeed, the evolving condition of the urban quality of life and what measures can be taken to enhance it, are relevant to the Urban Ski Mountain. Taking into account the scenario of an intensified cityscape, with increasing stresses on air quality, open space for leisure, and general feelings of well-being, the importance of these commodities are no longer being taken for granted.

With aim to develop a structured and controlled technical process, reactive to the evolutionary growth of various city conditions, the examination of biological constructs has provided a certain amount of technical influence for the scheme. Using the premise of performance, and through the study of a biological construct - the Heliconia plant form - a stacking system was derived and evolved in such a way as to react to varied parameters of densification, as well as various typological constraints and requirements. The collaboration of physical efficiency with the typological requirements of a structure for skiing gave a resultant set of optimum parameters. The gradual change in gradient as the structure becomes more vertical was greatly influenced and pre-determined through the investigation of skill level within the sport, as well as other factors of speed, route enjoyment and maximum lengths of runs.

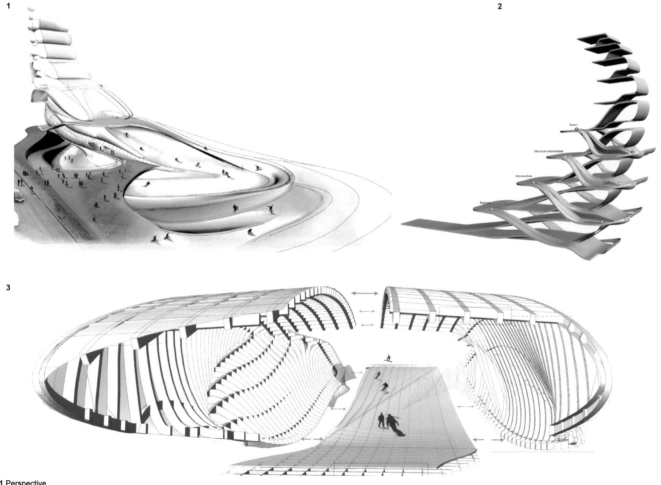

1 Perspective
2 Tracks diagram
3 Structure

1 ng south towards the city.

2

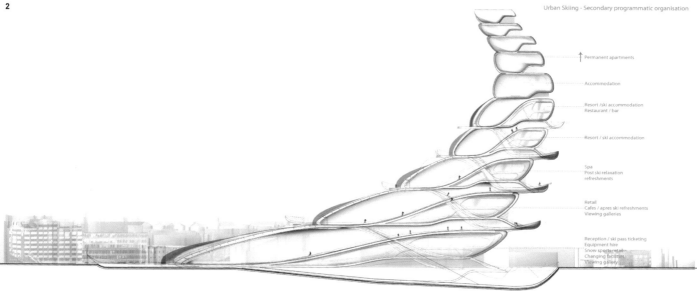

Urban Skiing - Secondary programmatic organisation

↑ Permanent apartments

Accommodation

Resort /ski accommodation
Restaurant / bar

Resort / ski accommodation

Spa
Post ski relaxation
refreshments

Retail
Cafes / apres ski refreshments
Viewing galleries

Reception / ski pass ticketing
Equipment hire
Snow sports retail
Changing facilities
Viewing gallery

1 View from street
2 Longitudinal section

Throughout history, mankind has been competing to build higher towers, not only to meet spacial demands, but also to celebrate and display their technological ability. Perhaps, this kind of proud achievement is interpreted as the origin of our desire towards vertical architecture. In this sense, one can say that every vertical structure has its own monumentality.

While a historical monumental tower speaks of certain memory or event, a contemporary skyscraper should celebrate its height, functions and achievement of technology. The depiction for monumentality of a skyscraper should be a different concept from the representation of a historical monument. Contemporary skyscrapers tend to express their grandiosity in a monotonous way, as if to mimic a historical monument. This kind of phenomena eventually leads a contemporary skyscraper to be perceived as mere vertical storage, void of historical significance or real technological achievement. This design proposal explores a skyscraper that denies mere representation of vertical emptiness and becomes an attractive feature to the public. In other words, the proposal aims at true monumentality, which appears when true architecture is in operation.

1

EVAPORATION PROCESS
Morphology of the building shape is derived from the mimics of water evaporation process. The water bubble-like spheres become sauna units as well as landscape ornaments on the deck.

2

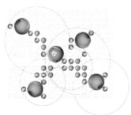

SKIN CONFIGURATION
From the simple pattern, each sauna unit is grouped as core+sauna units and configured its location. The configured pattern is projected into the skin. The unit groups sit on the punctuated holes of the skin.

1 Evaporation process
2 Skin configuration

The vertical spa facility, located at approximately 200 ft. of height, releases steam from each sauna unit, creating an elegant skin that covers the tower, simulating how humans sweat during physical activity. A sphere sauna shell and its integration with the core, are derived from the shape of pores in the skin. The vertical circulation and the elevator work as the skeleton of the facility. The framed glass is a depiction of covering drapery, as well as pathways for steam evaporation.

The facility is located on the river, so the environment creates the mirror image of the tower on the surface of water. The reflection of the tower and steam evaporation neutralize the heavy sense of gravity, as well as the sense of buoyancy. The deck with punctuated holes is filled with spherical ornaments and plants, which create a sense of continuity from the ground level to the top of the tower as if water bubbles floated from the river to the air. With maximum capable operation, the tower becomes a vertical connection between ground and sky.

1

2

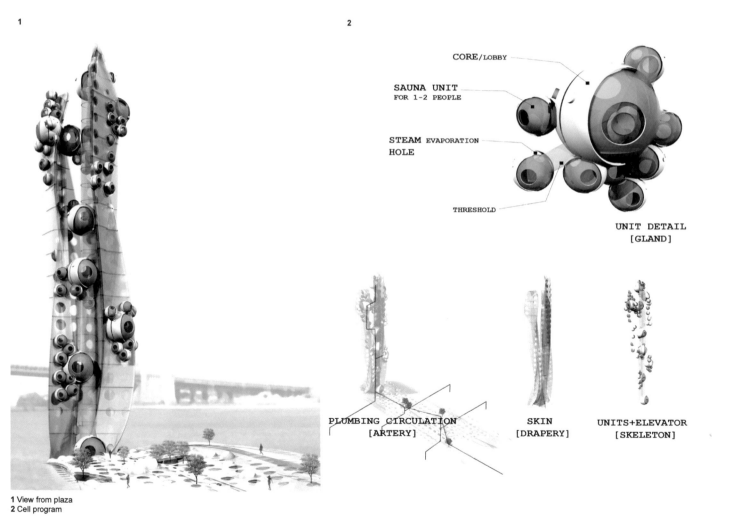

CORE/LOBBY

SAUNA UNIT
FOR 1-2 PEOPLE

STEAM EVAPORATION
HOLE

THRESHOLD

UNIT DETAIL
[GLAND]

PLUMBING CIRCULATION
[ARTERY]

SKIN
[DRAPERY]

UNITS+ELEVATOR
[SKELETON]

1 View from plaza
2 Cell program

The beginning of the 17th Century was the advent for the first trade routes. It was because of its great geographical position, that New York grew fast. After the Erie Canal was finished in 1825, it opened vast areas of New York to commerce and settlement. It was the wind which carried the first ships to this place and it was the beginning of its financial, cultural, and political development. Sailing ships were able to transfer trade goods via the Atlantic to Manhattan, and about the Hudson River to the vast areas of New York. The early historical background of New York is the main idea of this project. To combine the early seafaring with necessary methods to save energy is an important element. It should be a self-sufficient tower, constructed with light metal. The buildings' envelope should be able to catch the wind. A symbol of the early history of New York, which represents its energy-conscious future.

The Great Lakes, ocean, rivers, and mountains, give New York its characteristic weather. New York has a humid continental climate, resulting from prevailing wind patterns that bring cool air from the interior of the North American continent. Masses of cold, dry air frequently arrive from the northern interior of the continent. Prevailing winds from the South and Southwest transport warm, humid air. A further air mass flows inland from the North Atlantic Ocean and produces cool, cloudy, and damp weather conditions.

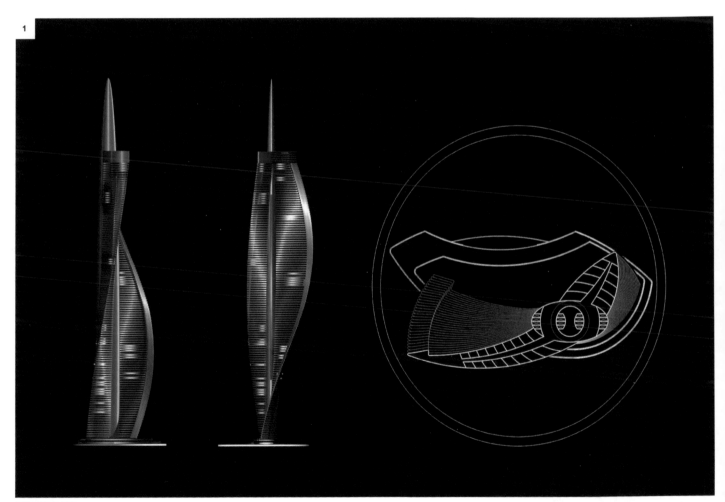

1

1 Elevations, plan

The "Wind Catcher Tower" is 560 meters high, and has 125 floors. It could be used for various activities; retail, offices, apartments, and penthouses. Some structural engineers define a high-rise as any vertical construction for which wind is a more significant load factor than weight. This is a good reason to design an aerodynamic skyscraper that is able to absorb the wind power and use it to produce electricity.

Built on a rotating platform, the tower is able to move into the right position, where its skin can catch the wind. The stream of wind would be channeled to the top, moving faster through the three wind-generators which are fixed in a vertical position on the last technical floor. The steel floors are attached to the central core, where elevators and emergency staircases are located. A climate control system could also be supported by the wind at the building's surface. The electricity for the moving platform would be provided by the self-sufficient tower, giving it the ability to move in a soft and slow manner.

A "Wind Tower" to move history into the future.

1 Perspective
2 View from plaza

>CARLO AIELLO studied architecture at the National Autonomous University of Mexico. He received a masters degree in Advanced Architectural Design from the Graduate School of Architecture, Planning and Preservation at Columbia University in 2004. He is founder and partner of eVolo Architecture. He previously worked at Asymptote Architecture and Skidmore, Owings, and Merrill.

LaVergne, TN USA
24 August 2009
1554LVUK00002B